Staging Favorites

Staging Favorites explores theatrical representations of royal favorites in Spanish, French, and English dramatic production during the late sixteenth and seventeenth centuries.

During this time, the courts of Spain, France, and England were dominated by all-powerful ministers who enjoyed royal favor. The politics of royal favoritism gave rise to a significant group of plays which constitutes the subject of this book. While scholars have studied this group partially and separately in national context, *Staging Favorites* approaches these "dramas about favorites" from a wider European point of view, and performs comparative analyses of a number of plays – including *La paciencia en la fortuna*; *Le Favori, ou la Coquette*; and *Sejanus His Fall* – and adds new detail and differentiation to the early modern perception and representation of the royal favorite.

This book will appeal to scholars and students interested in early modern literature, history of theater, and cultural history.

Francisco Gómez Martos holds a PhD in History from the Universidad Carlos III de Madrid, Spain, and a PhD in Spanish Literature from the Johns Hopkins University, USA. His main research interests are historiography and early modern culture.

Routledge Studies in Renaissance and Early Modern Worlds of Knowledge

Series Editors: Harald E. Braun (University of Liverpool) and Emily Michelson (University of St Andrews)

This series explores Renaissance and Early Modern Worlds of Knowledge (c.1400-c.1700) in Europe, the Americas, Asia and Africa. The volumes published in this series study the individuals, communities and networks involved in making and communicating knowledge during the first age of globalization. Authors investigate the perceptions, practices and modes of behaviour which shaped Renaissance and Early Modern intellectual endeavour and examine the ways in which they reverberated in the political, cultural, social and economic sphere.

The series is interdisciplinary, comparative and global in its outlook. We welcome submissions from new as well as existing fields of Renaissance Studies, including the history of literature (including neo-Latin, European and non-European languages), science and medicine, religion, architecture, environmental and economic history, the history of the book, art history, intellectual history and the history of music. We are particularly interested in proposals that straddle disciplines and are innovative in terms of approach and methodology.

The series includes monographs, shorter works and edited collections of essays. The Society for Renaissance Studies (http://www.rensoc.org.uk) provides an expert editorial board, mentoring, extensive editing and support for contributors to the series, ensuring high standards of peer-reviewed scholarship. We welcome proposals from early career researchers as well as more established colleagues.

14 Staging Favorites
Theatrical Representations of Political Favoritism in the Early Modern Courts of Spain, France, and England
Francisco Gómez Martos

For more information about this series, please visit: https://www.routledge.com/Routledge-Studies-in-Renaissance-and-Early-Modern-Worlds-of-Knowledge/book-series/ASHSER4043

Staging Favorites

Theatrical Representations of Political Favoritism in the Early Modern Courts of Spain, France, and England

Francisco Gómez Martos

Routledge
Taylor & Francis Group
LONDON AND NEW YORK

First published 2021
by Routledge
2 Park Square, Milton Park, Abingdon, Oxon OX14 4RN

and by Routledge
605 Third Avenue, New York, NY 10017

First issued in paperback 2022

Routledge is an imprint of the Taylor & Francis Group, an informa business

Publisher's Note
The publisher has gone to great lengths to ensure the quality of this reprint but points out that some imperfections in the original copies may be apparent.

British Library Cataloguing-in-Publication Data
A catalogue record for this book is available from the British Library

Library of Congress Cataloging-in-Publication Data
Names: Gómez Martos, Francisco, author.
Title: Staging favorites : theatrical representations of political favoritism in the early modern courts of Spain, France, and England / Francisco Gómez Martos.
Description: Abingdon, Oxon ; New York : Routledge, 2021. | Series: Routledge studies in Renaissance and early modern worlds of knowledge | Includes bibliographical references and index.
Identifiers: LCCN 2020015749 (print) | LCCN 2020015750 (ebook) | ISBN 9780367538415 (hardback) | ISBN 9781003083481 (ebook)
Subjects: LCSH: European drama—17th century—History and criticism. | Favorites, Royal, in literature. | Courts and courtiers in literature. | Authors and patrons—Europe—History—17th century. | Theater—Europe—History—17th century. | Europe—Courts and courtiers—History—17th century.
Classification: LCC PN1831. G66 2021 (print) | LCC PN1831. (ebook) | DDC 809.2/9352621—dc23
LC record available at https://lccn.loc.gov/2020015749
LC ebook record available at https://lccn.loc.gov/2020015750

ISBN: 978-0-367-53843-9 (pbk)
ISBN: 978-0-367-53841-5 (hbk)
ISBN: 978-1-003-08348-1 (ebk)

DOI: 10.4324/9781003083481

Typeset in Sabon
by codeMantra

To Anna

Contents

Introduction

In 1969 the sociologist Norbert Elias published a seminal work discussing what he called the "court society." He first questioned the conventional perspectives of an industrial society that had overlooked the social and historical significance of the etiquette and the symbolism surrounding the absolute monarch and, by extension, the functioning of the royal court. Elias then made clear that during the early modern age, the king was the main source of power, and the court, the place where the royal household with its countless dependents was located, was the primary destination for people seeking favors, influence, and status. The ultimate goal of these people living at court was therefore being as close as possible to the king and enjoying the honor and favors that were associated with that position.

This court society, during the late sixteenth and seventeenth centuries, witnessed the emergence of court favorites, all-powerful ministers who enjoyed royal favor in its greatest form. In the courts of Spain, France, and England these royal favorites, at the apex of the pyramid of power, used their privileged position to monopolize relations of patronage and lead extensive networks of clients, ranging from the favorite's most immediate subordinate to the most miserable poet who hoped to obtain some sort of reward by serving as an entertainer and propagandist for his patron. The rise of favorite ministers coincided with the exponential growth of urban population in those cities hosting a court, such as Madrid, Paris, and London, and the subsequent growth of the play-going public and the transformation of the theater into an exceptional channel for cultural expression.[1]

Throughout this period, numerous playwrights composed dramas featuring favorite ministers and commenting on political favoritism. Just as there are multiple names for the figure of the royal favorite – among the most frequently used are *valido* and *privado* in Spanish, *favori* in French, and "favorite" and "private" in English–, scholars also employ various terms to describe the plays dealing with the phenomenon of royal favoritism, which in Spanish is usually known as *valimiento* or *privanza* and in French as *ministériat*. Those plays are generally known in Spanish as *dramas* or *comedias de privanza*, and in French, the expression *drames des favoris* has been used sporadically for the same purpose.[2] In English, despite the numerous dramas focused on the role of the favorite written in the Tudor and Stuart courts, there is no standard designation for these plays. Henceforth, the concept "dramas on favorites," which is amply discussed in Chapter 1, will be used globally to refer to any play exploring the topic of royal favoritism.

***

Scholars still discuss whether the early modern models of royal favoritism are a unique phenomenon in history or, on the contrary, they occur in other periods as well. This debate receives considerable attention in *The World of the Favourite*, a collaborative book edited by John Elliott and Laurence Brockliss. Centered on the kingdoms of Spain, France, and England in the sixteenth and seventeenth centuries, this book supports "the singularity of the minister-favourite" (280) roughly between 1550 and 1650.[3] After the publication of *The World of the Favourite* in the late 1990s, new studies have tried to expand in different ways the definition of the early modern favorite minister. Among the most recent contributions, one must mention the proceedings of a conference held in Germany in 2002. Edited by Jan Hirschbiegel and Werner Paravicini and published under the title *Der Fall des Günstlings: Hofparteien in Europa vom 13. bis zum 17. Jahrhundert*, the papers forming this volume point to the long-term phenomenon of royal favoritism, which is seen as a structural element of the monarchies already existing in the Middle Ages.[4] The study of royal favorites in medieval Europe, however, is not the only remarkable contribution of this book. More importantly, *Der Fall des Günstlings* draws attention to the practice of favoritism in a large part of Europe and to particular aspects thereof such as the importance of clientelism for the favorites' existence. In addition to these latter contributions, Francesco Benigno, in his study *Favoriti e ribelli* (2011), points out that there are certain resemblances between the seventeenth-century models of political favoritism practiced by monarchs and their ministers and the struggle for and distribution of power within the papacy during the same period of time. In the Roman court, the relevance of the Secretary of State and the practice of nepotism, which had a long tradition in the papacy, experienced a notable escalation throughout the seventeenth century in coincidence with the heyday of favorite ministers in the European monarchies (83–97). In summary, ongoing studies are extending the scope of the topic of political favoritism beyond the most powerful Western European monarchies of the early modern age on which historiography has traditionally focused.

This tradition also includes numerous studies focused on the representation of royal favorites in literary works. For instance, some of the scholarly volumes mentioned earlier, such as *The World of the Favourite*, contain essays on the presence of royal favorites in the arts and specifically in literature and drama. In this regard, Curtis Perry's analysis of what he calls the "discourse of favoritism" in early modern England is a contribution of great significance. Starting from the 1580s, that discourse runs for sixty years and includes several kinds of writing such as chronicles, poems, prose fictions, pamphlets, parliamentary speeches, and of course plays, which constitute the main focus of Perry's research. Similar to Perry's approach is the dissertation of Delphine Amstutz on *La Fable du favori* in seventeenth-century French literature, including different types of texts such as libels, sermons, dedications, and panegyrics, in addition to the most established literary genres, prose fiction, poetry, and drama.[5] In the case of the Spanish letters, in contrast to the English and French, there is a lack of works dealing with the topic of royal favoritism in literature altogether; in other words, no scholar has analyzed, as a whole, an extensive corpus of literary Spanish texts similar to those explored by Perry and Amstutz.[6]

When the focus is narrowed specifically to theatrical representations of favorites, the state of the field in Spanish drama also differs from its French and English counterparts. In this case, the multiple monographs and articles dedicated to the examination of *comedias de privanza* as a group[7] contrast with the scarce studies discussing French or English dramas on favorites in general.[8] It is likewise rare to find approaches to the subject of royal favoritism in theater across languages and nations. Furthermore, the studies that analyze dramas on favorites from an international point of view are not only rare, but they are also limited to the comparison of specific Spanish plays to either French or English pieces of theater.[9] A more inclusive analysis, however, has never been accomplished.

***

This book, by analyzing and comparing a selection of Spanish, French, and English dramas on favorites, aims to contribute to filling that void of international studies. In addition, the present work contributes to the study of theatrical representations of favorites by discussing a recently discovered play concerning favoritism, *La paciencia en la fortuna*. In the course of my archival research, I came across this seventeenth-century Spanish drama that remains unedited and, as I recently argued, was written by the famed Lope de Vega (Gómez, "La paciencia"). After a preliminary research of the two surviving manuscript copies of the play, I realized that *La paciencia en la fortuna*, which features a royal favorite, was of extraordinary interest for my project due to several reasons. First, this play illustrates clearly how Spanish dramatists used to depict royal favorites by remarking on their positive virtues, which in the case of *La paciencia en la fortuna* is primarily the protagonist's patience. Moreover, this play is also a typical example of the confluence between political favoritism and literary patronage at court, given that the author of *La paciencia en la fortuna* praises and receives favors from the Duke of Lerma, King Philip III's royal favorite.

More importantly, some of the themes that *La paciencia en la fortuna* examines are shared with other dramas on favorites written in the early modern courts of France and England. For instance, the stoicism of the protagonist of *La paciencia en la fortuna* refers to a greater body of values and ideas known as Neostoicism, which was widespread in Western Europe during the sixteenth and seventeenth centuries and worked as a framework for portraying royal favorites. This circumstance places *La paciencia en la fortuna* into a wider framework and allows a comprehensive approach and a comparative study of this play with other European dramas. With this purpose, for the analysis of this book, two other plays, Marie-Catherine Desjardins' *Le Favori, ou la Coquette* and Ben Jonson's *Sejanus His Fall*, have been chosen due not only to their significance as extraordinary examples of French and English dramas on favorites but also to the topics that they cover and the possibility to compare them to *La paciencia en la fortuna*.

These motivations explain the structure of this book and the order of its chapters. Chapter 1 offers a general analysis of the emergence and development of dramas on favorites in Spain, France, and England, with an emphasis on the historical context and the theoretical components defining these dramas. The next three chapters focus on the *mise en scène* of favorite ministers in each of those three countries separately. Each chapter comprises an overview of the representation of favorites in Spanish, French, and English drama, respectively, and an in-depth analysis of a play: *La paciencia en la fortuna*, *Le Favori, ou la Coquette*, and *Sejanus His Fall*, respectively. The main factor guiding the order of the chapters is the relation of *La paciencia en la fortuna* to the other dramas on favorites, more notably its similarities with *Le Favori, ou la Coquette* and its differences with *Sejanus His Fall*. In turn, the progression from the chapter on Spanish drama to the subsequent chapters on French and English drama also shows the influence that the *comedias de privanza* had on the *drames des favoris* as well as the importance that French politics and literature, including drama, had on the appearance of favorite characters on the English stage. In any case, each of the three chapters stands on its own and can be read separately. The results of the whole analysis are integrated into a final conclusion that compares the different treatments of the topic of political favoritism in theater and underlines some of the main features of dramas on favorites.

Notes

1 On the impact of the increasing urban population on the baroque literature, see Maravall, especially Chapter 4.
2 Delphine Amstutz widely uses the term *drame du favori*, which she borrows from Steve Uomini (Amstutz, *La Fable du favori*, esp. 87).
3 Previous historiography pointed toward this same direction. See the works of Bérenger and Tomás y Valiente.
4 This approach can be also seen in the volume *Los validos* (edited by J. A. Escudero), which focuses on royal favoritism in the history of Spain.

5 I wish to thank Professor Delphine Amstutz for sending me an electronic copy of her dissertation.
6 Two exceptions are the volumes edited by Tropé (*La représentation du favori dans l'Espagne de Philippe III et de Philippe IV*) and Matas Caballero et al. (*El Duque de Lerma: Poder y literatura en el Siglo de Oro*), which nevertheless cover the topic in an unevenly dispersed and irregular way. For instance, half of the studies included in *El Duque de Lerma* focus on the poet Luis de Góngora and his unfinished panegyric to Lerma.
7 See especially Cauvin, MacCurdy, Peale, Ferrer, Profeti, and Wise.
8 See Amstutz ("Favoris et conseillers") and Worden, respectively.
9 For the comparison between some Spanish and French dramas on favorites, see Gethner ("Power Grabbing" and "Love and Friendship"), Bauer-Funke, and Teulade; as for Spanish and English dramas, see the works of Bradner and Feros.

Works Cited

Amstutz, Delphine. "Favoris et conseillers sur là scene tragique du premier XVIIe siècle." *Dramaturgies du conseil et de la délibération*, edited by Xavier Bonnier and Ariane Ferry, CÉRÉdI, Actes de colloques et journées d'étude, no. 16, 2016, pp. 1–9, accessed 20 March, 2020, http://ceredi.labos.univ-rouen.fr/public/?favoris-et-conseillers-sur-la.html

———. *La Fable du favori dans la littérature française du premier XVIIe siècle*. Dissertation, Université Paris-Sorbonne, 2013.

Bauer-Funke, Cerstin. "Análisis comparado de *El ejemplo mayor de la desdicha* de Antonio Mira de Amescua y *Bélisaire* de Jean Rotrou." *Actas del V Congreso Internacional de la Asociación Internacional Siglo de Oro (AISO)*, edited by Christoph Strosetzki, Iberoamericana, 2001, pp. 176–86.

Benigno, Francesco. *Favoriti e ribelli: Stili della politica baroca*. Bulzoni, 2011.

Bérenger, Jean. "Pour une enquête européenne: le problème du ministériat au XVIIe siècle." *Annales*, vol. 29, no. 1, 1974, pp. 166–92.

Bradner, Leicester. "The Theme of *privanza* in Spanish and English Drama 1590–1625." *Homenaje a William L. Fichter. Estudios sobre teatro antiguo hispánico y otros ensayos*, edited by A. David Kossoff and José Amor, Castalia, 1971, pp. 97–106.

Cauvin, Mary Austin. *The comedia de privanza in the seventeenth century*. Dissertation, U of Pennsylvania, 1957.

Desjardins, Marie-Catherine (Madame de Villedieu). *Le Favori*. Edited by Delphine Amstutz, Hermann, 2017.

Elias, Norbert. *La sociedad cortesana*. 1969. 2nd ed. Fondo de Cultura Económica, 2012.

Elliott, John, and Laurence Brockliss, editors. *The World of the Favourite*. Yale UP, 1999.

Escudero, José Antonio, editor. *Los validos*. Universidad Rey Juan Carlos, 2004.

Feros, Antonio. "Historia y poesía: monarcas y favoritos en las obras de Marlowe y Mira de Amescua." *Del poder y sus críticos en el mundo ibérico del Siglo de Oro*, edited by I. Arellano et al., Iberoamericana-Vervuert, 2013, pp. 111–42.

Ferrer Valls, Teresa. "El juego del poder: Lope de Vega y los dramas de la privanza." *Modelos de vida en la España del Siglo de Oro*, vol. 1, edited by I. Arellano and M. Vitse, Iberoamericana, 2004, pp. 159–85.

Gethner, Perry. "Love and Friendship: From Tirso to Desjardins." *Papers on French Seventeenth Century Literature*, vol. 32, no. 62, 2005, pp. 113–24.

———. "Power Grabbing and Court Opportunism: From Spain to France." *Echoes and Inscriptions: Comparative Approaches to Early Modern Spanish Literatures*, edited by Barbara Simerka and Christopher Weimer, Bucknell UP, 2000, pp. 120–8.

Gómez Martos, Francisco. "*La paciencia en la fortuna*: An Unprinted Play by Lope de Vega." *Arte nuevo. Revista de estudios áureos*, vol. 6, 2019, pp. 57–89.

Hirschbiegel, Jan, and Werner Paravicini, editors. *Der Fall des Günstlings: Hofparteien in Europa vom 13. bis zum 17. Jahrhundert*. Jan Thorbecke Verlag, 2004.

Jonson, Ben. *Sejanus His Fall*. Edited by Tom Cain. *The Cambridge Edition of the Works of Ben Jonson*, 7 vols., edited by D. Bevington et al., Cambridge UP, 2012, vol. 2, pp. 195–391.

La paciencia en la fortuna. 1615. MS 16459. Biblioteca Nacional de España, Madrid. 1–56v.

La paciencia en la fortuna. CC*IV 28033, *Comedias de Diferentes Autores*, vol. 74, no. 2. Biblioteca Palatina di Parma, Parma. 1–55r.

MacCurdy, Raymond. *The Tragic Fall: Don Álvaro de Luna and Other Favorites in Spanish Golden Age Drama*. U of North Carolina P, 1978.

Maravall, José Antonio. *La cultura del Barroco: Análisis de una estructura histórica*. Ariel, 1975.

Matas Caballero, Juan et al. *El Duque de Lerma: Poder y literatura en el Siglo de Oro*. Centro de Estudios Europa Hispánica, 2011.

Peale, C. George. "Comienzos, enfoques y constitución de la comedia de privanza en la *Tercera parte de las comedias de Lope de Vega y otros auctores*." *Hispanic Review*, vol. 72, no. 1, 2004, pp. 125–56.

Perry, Curtis. *Literature and Favoritism in Early Modern England*. Cambridge UP, 2006.

Profeti, María G. "Funciones teatrales y literarias del personaje del privado." Tropé, pp. 113–29.

Teulade, Anne. "Le théâtre du doble: la réception de la *Comedia de privanza* entre tragédie et tragi-comédie." *Le théâtre espagnol du Siècle d'Or en France (XVIIe-XXe siècle). De la traduction au transfert culturel*, edited by Christophe Couderc, Presses Universitaires de Paris Ouest, 2012, pp. 101–15.

Tomás y Valiente, Francisco. *Los validos en la monarquía española del siglo XVII: Estudio institucional*. 1982. 2nd ed. Instituto de Estudios Políticos, 1990.

Tropé, Hélène, editor. *La représentation du favori dans l'Espagne de Philippe III et de Philippe IV*. Presses Sorbonne nouvelle, 2010.

Wise, Carl. *Shadow of the King: Privanza and Perceptions of Royal Power in Seventeenth-Century Spanish Theater*. Dissertation, U of Georgia, 2011.

Worden, Blair. "Favourites on the English Stage." Elliott and Brockliss, pp. 159–83.

1 Dramas on favorites

History and theory

From the late sixteenth century to the second half of the seventeenth century, there exists a significant number of Spanish, French, and English dramas dealing with the topic of political favoritism to consider them part of the same group. In Spain there exist at least sixty-five dramas featuring favorites as their main character (Peale, "Comienzos" 129, n. 13), in England upward of fifty (Perry 3), and in France, with the lowest number, one can count no fewer than forty (Amstutz, *La Fable du favori* 361–452), bringing the total number of dramas on favorites from those three countries to over 150. To this number, furthermore, one could add the plays in which favorite ministers play a less central but nonetheless relevant role, such as the character Diego Tenorio, father to the protagonist of *El burlador de Sevilla* (c.1621), and the representations of all-powerful ministers in other types of dramatic performances such as *autos sacramentales* (one-act allegorical dramas) in Spain, court ballets in France, and court masques in England. Finally, some dramas concerned with royal favoritism, for example *Henry the Una* (c.1619) (Steggle 119–32), are still lost and it remains as a task for future research to trace their whereabouts.[1] In recent years, new dramas on favorites have been edited and studied, for instance *The Emperor's Favourite* (c.1629) (Keenan) and *La paciencia en la fortuna* (c. 1612) (Gómez, "La paciencia").

The magnitude of this group of plays makes it exceptionally difficult to produce a concise and inclusive definition of dramas on favorites. To my knowledge, no scholar has ever attempted to propose a definition for this transnational and multilingual corpus, and the theories elaborated by those who have focused on the theater of one country are far from exhaustive and cannot be applied to other contexts. For instance, regarding Spanish drama, scholars disagree about whether Spanish plays dealing with the topic of favoritism qualify as a dramatic genre in itself[2] or rather as a subgenre dependent on the so-called "genealogical drama," dramas intended to exalt certain lineages.[3] This last theory, developed by Teresa Ferrer and generally supported by scholars,[4] is based almost wholly on the analysis of Lope de Vega's dramatic work and therefore fails to include numerous plays on the same topic written by other dramatists such as Luis Vélez de

Guevara (Crivellari), Antonio Mira de Amescua (Arellano 57–82), Tirso de Molina (Albrecht 127–67), Juan Ruiz de Alarcón (Halpern 73–120; Campbell; Peale, "Los principios"), Francisco de Quevedo (Fernández Mosquera), Calderón de la Barca (Sáez), or Juan Pérez de Montalbán.[5] Due to the narrowness of this scope, some of the common elements that Ferrer finds in the dramas on favorites, such as the setting in Hispanic courts and the playwrights' intentions of praising the genealogy of noble families, can hardly be seen in Spanish dramas featuring favorites like the Roman Sejanus (Pérez de Montalbán's *Amor, privanza y castigo*, c. 1621) or the English Earl of Essex (Coello's *El Conde de Sex*, 1633), and certainly they are not applicable to most French and English dramas on favorites either.

A more inclusive analysis of the political favoritism theme in Spanish drama is provided by Caparrós ("Privado") and Peale ("Comienzos"), although their definitions would be to a great extent inefficacious for identifying and analyzing themes and patterns of French and English dramas on favorites. For instance, the gradual development of the favorite character that Amstutz traces throughout the first half of seventeenth-century French drama ("Favoris et conseillers"), starting with the traditional figure of the royal counselor that is common in the first decades of the century and progressively replaced by the prevalent character of the favorite minister in the age of Richelieu, does not seem to be relevant for Spanish and English drama, in which the emergence of all-powerful ministers as main characters is more abrupt, consistent, and concentrated within a shorter period of time. In turn, the use of sodomy and disorderly sexual behavior that is a typical symbol for transgression of power in many favorite characters in English drama is rarely seen in Spanish and French plays. For that same reason, the topics discussed in the works of Worden ("Favourites") and Perry, which are probably the most thorough studies of the favoritism phenomenon in English theater, have limited application to dramatic contexts on the continent.

Finally, there are only a few studies with an international focus on the theatrical representations of royal favoritism and they are limited to the comparison of certain Spanish plays and playwrights to their French and English counterparts. For instance, Bradner and Feros ("Historia y poesía"), focusing on the works of Antonio Mira de Amescua and Christopher Marlowe, emphasize the dissimilarities in the way Spanish and English playwrights portray favorite ministers and underline that the favorable and positive depiction of dramatic favorites in Spain contrasts with the more critical and negative representations of their English counterparts.[6] Although this interpretation, as a whole, seems arguably accurate, one must take into consideration that in early modern England there also exists a literary discourse endorsing favoritism that is reflected in a significant number of dramas such as the anonymous *True Chronicle History of the Whole Life and Death of Thomas Lord Cromwell* (1600) or Lodowick Carlell's *The Deserving Favourite* (c. 1627).[7] To this important qualification, in turn, one may also add that Spanish drama has examples of favorites who are far from heroic and virtuous and in which the practice of favoritism is questioned, for example, in *El Duque de Viseo* (c. 1608) by Lope de Vega or *La confusión de Hungría* by Mira de Amescua.[8]

In sum, given the great heterogeneity with which dramatists from across Western Europe deal with the topic of political favoritism, one is in a way forced to define dramas on favorites in the most concise but flexible way possible, so that the categorization of those dramas allows us to include a wide selection of plays. With this aim in mind, dramas on favorites are essentially those dramas featuring someone in the sovereign's highest favor as the protagonist and focused on the issues that are associated with that position. This unadorned definition, nonetheless, ignores dramas in which favorite ministers are not the main character and isolates dramas on favorites from plays whose storylines involve issues resulting from political favoritism. *La Estrella de Sevilla* (c. 1623), for example, is never included in the group of Spanish *comedias de privanza* because it focuses on the figure of King Sancho and the problems that his irresponsible love affairs cause among the Castilian nobility. The king's right-hand man, Arias, participates in the play but he is neither in the stage's spotlight nor is the royal favoritism theme primarily discussed. However, there is little doubt that Arias, who makes decisions for the king, plays the traditional role of the influential favorite minister as seen in contemporary dramas focusing on this political figure. Furthermore, based on historical events that can be correlated to events of the play – King Philip IV's visit to Seville in 1624 –, it has been argued that, within the traditional framework of a play focused on love and royal loyalty, *La Estrella de Sevilla* hides a critical message against Philip IV and his favorite, the Count-Duke of Olivares (Sieber, "Cloaked History"). Similarly, Philip Massinger's *Maid of Honour* (c. 1621) features a secondary character, the corrupt minion Fulgentio, who may well be a characterization of King James I's favorite, the Duke of Buckingham (Worden, "Favourites" 172 and Keenan 297).

These examples suggest that the absence, in certain plays, of a favorite minister as the main character does not completely diminish the value of those plays as theatrical representations of royal favoritism. Further, there exist dramas in which the character of the royal favorite is apparently absent and yet these plays may indirectly comment on the contemporary topic of favoritism under their present circumstances. For example, in Lope's *El caballero de Olmedo* (c. 1621), there is no explicit royal favorite, but the drama takes place during the reign of King John II of Castile, in the fifteenth century, and one of the characters is an unnamed constable. As was well known in Lope's times, John II's reign was marked by two powerful constables, Ruy López Dávalos and especially Álvaro de Luna, who were characterized as royal favorites in multiple Spanish dramas during the seventeenth century. In *El caballero de Olmedo*, the constable character seems irrelevant for the flow of the dramatic action and he barely participates in it, but given his presence, one can argue that Lope has in mind the favorites of his own time. This is one of the conversations between the king and the constable:

"KING: Don't bring me affairs to resolve,
As I'm leaving.
CONSTABLE: They only require your signature,
You needn't be troubled with the particulars." (2.1554–7)[9]

This scenario is reminiscent of early seventeenth-century Spain when monarchs delegated to a great extent the management of the government to their chief ministers while they spent a significant amount of time on activities such as hunting. Contemporary drama, as the quatrain cited earlier suggests, regularly reflected this anomalous situation.

To *El caballero de Olmedo* one might add numerous other examples of plays apparently unrelated to royal favoritism that have however been influenced by this topic. For instance, *Volpone* (c. 1605), arguably Ben Jonson's best comedy, presents an acidic parody of early modern English society based on patron-client associations. The turbulent relationship between its protagonists, the master Volpone and his parasite Mosca, may be compared to that of a ruler with his favorite. Indeed, this play is immediately preceded by Jonson's *Sejanus His Fall* (c.1603) and the two works have been read together: whereas *Sejanus His Fall* dramatizes the relation between Emperor Tiberius and his minion Sejanus, in *Volpone* that relation is transferred to a lower rank of society.[10]

If dramas without a royal favorite character, as clearly shown in the case of *Volpone*, may be relevant for the theatrical representation of royal favoritism, inversely, the presence of monarchs and favorite ministers as protagonists of dramas does not always indicate that the dramas in question explore kingship and favoritism within an early modern political frame. Indeed, in this epoch, there are plays that use the omnipresent figure of the royal favorite and the language associated with this privileged and controversial position to delve deeper into leitmotivs, such as love and faith, with no intention or priority to comment on the political context in which those plays are composed. For example, Mira de Amescua's *El arpa de David* (c. 1612) dramatizes David's rise to favor in Saul's court according to elements that are characteristic of dramas on favorites during the same period, focusing on the vicissitudes experienced by a royal favorite who generates both admiration and jealousy. However, in spite of some anachronistic features and the introduction of elements invented by Amescua in order to make an entertaining performance for the seventeenth-century Spanish audience, the playwright closely follows the biblical account of David's story and his play does not attempt to serve as political commentary, but rather aims to highlight the value of Divine Providence by means of David's steady belief in God (Cauvin 208–14). Likewise, throughout the first half of seventeenth century, French dramatists tended to depict the lives of saints with features that were typical of royal favorites, thus transferring the relationship of the latter to their monarchs to that between saints or martyrs and God. This particular type of hagiographic drama, which is heavily influenced by images of royal favoritism, becomes a better-defined dramatic formula through the plays of Pierre Bello, Balthasar Baro, and Desfontaines, focused on the martyrdom of St. Eustace and published during the 1630s and early 1640s, thus contemporary with Cardinal Richelieu's government (Amstutz, *La Fable du favori* 407–12).

At this point of our analysis of theatrical representations of favorites, it becomes clear that the mere examination of the dramatic form of plays featuring favorites is insufficient, not only for comprehending the diversity and multiple themes of those plays but also in understanding their emergence and appreciating their significance in literary and historical contexts. In order to achieve a fuller comprehension of the large group of dramas on favorites, which for the most part is simultaneously produced in Spain, France, and England during the late sixteenth and seventeenth centuries, it is indispensable to take into consideration the historical circumstances and the intellectual components that seem to have been a common background for all those dramas. This perspective would allow us to delve into some of the elements shared by dramas on favorites across Western Europe. For instance, this approach could explain the sense of immediacy and political purport that is characteristic of dramas on favorites in a first phase, and the evolution of the favorite minister on stage from a primarily political and public figure to a more melodramatic and introspective character. This general evolution seems to be a pattern in drama in Spain (MacCurdy 220–1), France (Amstutz, *La Fable du favori* 361–452), and England (Worden, "Favourites"). In each of these countries, the appearance of favorites on stage coincides with the emergence of royal favoritism as an institutional phenomenon and a source of political debate. In this first phase of staging favorites, playwrights make good use of the popularity of the topic to exploit the dramatic opportunities offered by the figure of the favorite minister. Some of the earliest dramas written in this period, such as Salucio del Poyo's *La privanza y caída de Don Álvaro de Luna* (c. 1601) and Marlowe's *Edward II* (c. 1592), have a lasting impact on the development of this type of drama. However, in early modern theater, which is fueled by novelties, fashions become old rapidly. Consequently, even when royal favoritism remains firmly established in the political sphere, especially in Spain and France under the governments of the Count-Duke of Olivares and Cardinal Mazarin, respectively, and less in England during the Caroline era, the character of the favorite loses much of its initial freshness and becomes progressively less involved in political action. Late dramas like *La privanza desleal y voluntad por la fama* (1620s), Ford's *The Broken Heart* (c. 1633), and Desjardins' *Le Favori, ou la Coquette* (1664) feature stereotypical images of royal favorites absorbed in romantic and psychological matters and less engaged in the political and social issues related to their positions.

The aim of the remainder of this chapter, far from being an attempt to produce a definition able to encompass the development of the diverse group of dramas on favorites throughout the early modern age, is to delve into the historical and intellectual context in which those dramas are created as well as some of their most often-occurring themes.

Royal favoritism and playwriting

The concentration of dramas focusing on the theme of political favoritism during the late sixteenth and seventeenth centuries coincides naturally with the height of royal favorites in Europe. In Spain, the Duke of Lerma and the Count-Duke of Olivares are the omnipotent ministers who dominate politics while theatrical representations of favoritism develop. In this regard, the government of the Duke of Lerma is particularly significant, because, among other reasons, his rise to power in 1598 and the years immediately after his fall in 1618 mark the greatest era of Spanish dramas on favorites. Moreover, Lerma is an extraordinary patron of the arts and his appearance on the political scene propels a tremendous expansion of theater in Spain. In contrast to the years in which Lerma was the king's favorite and favors and rewards circulated profusely, Olivares' "relative parsimony in the dispensing of patronage" was accompanied by attempts to reduce spending and the flow of favors, thus making it impossible for him "to imitate the profligacy of his predecessor."[11]

The importance of Lerma's artistic patronage went beyond the Spanish territories. The Duke set a pattern as patron of the arts, especially architecture, sculpture, and painting, in the first half of the seventeenth century, an epoch of lavish spending for the European courts. His collection of paintings was one of the largest of his day and was unparalleled in Spain. He was, in the words of Sarah Schroth, "the first royal 'favorite' in Europe to collect pictures as a manifestation of power," and his example might have been followed by other royal favorites like the Duke of Buckingham and Cardinal Richelieu (99–100).

There is no doubt that Lerma was acknowledged by his contemporaries as the model royal minister and a pivotal politician on the European map. Simon Contarini, the Venetian ambassador to Spain, reported that Italian rulers used to send gifts, such as jewelry, to flatter and find favor with Lerma (569). A similar scene can be seen in England, from where the Duke also received gifts and where he had as his own pensioners the Howards and their clients, who were, in turn, allies of the English favorite the Earl of Somerset. King James I admired the exceptionality of Lerma as a minister and possibly had him in mind when he concentrated all royal favor upon Somerset (Peck, "Monopolizing" 59). Lerma may have served as a model for Somerset, but especially for his successor in the position of

James' favorite, the Duke of Buckingham, who in 1623 traveled to Spain and visited Lerma's art collection at La Ribera in Valladolid (Schroth 99).

This communication between the Spanish and English courts helps to explain why the governments of Lerma and Buckingham bear numerous resemblances.[12] First, the two favorites transformed the system of patronage and the distribution of royal bounty into a market monopolized by the dukes themselves. By concentrating favor and influence in the hands of an all-powerful minister, the monarch ceased to be the focus of patronage and competition at court decreased. This is what occurred in the Spanish and English courts when Lerma and Buckingham came to lead the networks, which could involve hundreds and thousands of people (Morgan 24), through whom royal bounty circulated. As such, the Dukes controlled the administration of favors, noble titles, and appointments to public offices. Seeking their own benefits as Lerma and Buckingham did, it is no surprise that corruption was rampant in the courts dominated by these all-powerful ministers. As an example, the years in which Lerma and Buckingham ruled coincide with an exponential growth of the nobility in both Spain and England, for the two favorites benefited from the distributions of those new titles. The courts of Spain and England at this period were true markets where titles, honors, and offices were continually traded in a business involving patrons and clients from top to bottom. The orchestrators of this business, Lerma and Buckingham, were repeatedly engaged in questionable transactions and were eventually accused of extortion, nepotism, and misappropriation of the royal treasury.

The situation in French politics throughout the seventeenth century is similar to that of Spain and England.[13] The royal patronage was exclusively directed toward favorite ministers to the detriment of the great nobles and powerful factions at court, which originated the monopolization of favor in the hands of all-powerful ministers and their own networks. Cardinal Richelieu was without a doubt the most distinguished French favorite of this time, and his lasting legacy was continued by his ministerial successors throughout the second half of the seventeenth century. Richelieu succeeded in forming a centralized and solid clientele connecting Paris with the rest of the provinces around the country. To do this, he embezzled large amounts of money from the royal coffers to reward his clients and showered them with titles, offices, and pensions. Through this clientele, Richelieu was able to extend his power and gain support for his projects and goals. As a result, he enjoyed and dispensed royal favor without competition for many years. During this time, he – like his successor Cardinal Mazarin – amassed an immense fortune, and so did his family and closest clients and court supporters.

This rapid and extraordinary enrichment was a common feature among royal favorites across Western Europe. Nevertheless, despite their tremendous wealth, some favorites like Lerma and Richelieu made wide use of their treasures and left behind debts by the end of their lives. This pattern illustrates the extravagance of seventeenth-century European courts. In this period, status and power were visual phenomena (Soria). One's position within a court society, as Elias argues, was determinant to enjoying certain privileges, and one gained that position, secured it, and met the requirements that came with it by making it visible. Instead of being accumulated and hidden, power was displayed ostentatiously. Given that one spent according to one's status and obligations, royal favorites were expected and even forced to display publicly their dominance over the rest of the courtiers. For instance, the Duke of Lerma, whose expenses on patronage surpassed in many aspects those of King Philip III, was required by the religious Order of Santiago that he represented to make regular contributions – a fifth of his possessions – to the churches and convents that he patronized (Banner).

These dynamics of expenses made the court look like a fountain of wealth flowing unceasingly (Sieber, "The Magnificent Fountain"). Banquets, clothes, jewelry, court spectacles, and buildings, to name a few, were part of the opulent spending that courtiers regularly carried out to fulfill the expectations of their status. A substantial portion of this wealth was destined for the production of literary and artistic works, thus attracting the arrival at court of a large number of artists and writers of every kind, including of course playwrights, who sought to benefit from the circulation of wealth and favors. A painter like Peter Rubens, for example, traveled around the courts of Europe, including the Spanish, French, and English courts, and contrived to portray some of the most important favorites of the day such as Lerma, Buckingham, and Olivares. Dramaturgy had no writer who, like Rubens, visited courts abroad and staged favorites internationally, but contemporary playwrights from different countries produced their dramatic works under similar circumstances and fueled by the same source: the financial support of court favorites. Famed theater figures like Lope de Vega, Luis Vélez de Guevara, Pierre Corneille, Jean de Rotrou, Christopher Marlowe, and Ben Jonson were among those dramatists who benefited extensively from the favorites' patronage.

Not only dramatists like the ones mentioned earlier who were well-known and enjoyed the direct patronage of a favorite minister benefited from the phenomenon of royal favoritism, but it seems that theater as a whole, in Spain, France, and England, experienced a notable advancement upon the ascension of all-powerful ministers. The greatest epochs of theater in those countries, especially Spain and England, coincided with the heydays of their respective royal favorites. These phases took place in Spain and England at the turn of the seventeenth century, the age of Lope de Vega and Shakespeare, and in France a few decades later, the age of Corneille. This coincidence, rather than being accidental, corresponds, in general, to the situation of the European courts that were dominated by all-powerful ministers and also, more specifically, to the favorite ministers' desire to use theater as a means of propaganda.

In this regard, the figure of Cardinal Richelieu was exemplary. No other decade in seventeenth-century France was more fruitful in producing new plays than the 1630s, the core years of Richelieu's *ministère*, and his loss in 1642 was followed by a general decline of theatrical activity and the abandonment of playwriting by certain dramatists (Lough, "The Earnings" 323–5). Richelieu, aside from being a playwright himself, promoted theater in different ways. Mainly, he standardized the theatrical practice by creating the Académie Française, an official institution providing financial support to dramatists and recognizing their work as a profession. In a more private sphere, he sponsored certain plays and playwrights and reserved a room at his Palais-Cardinal designated specifically for dramatic performances. The works on which he commented and those that he commissioned were not only dramas but essays about theory of theater as well, thus contributing to the development of dramatic criticism when such a field was still unknown in France (Mesnard 200; Couton 90). One of those essays was the *Projet pour le rétablissement du théâtre français* (1641, published later together with *La pratique du théâtre*), written by François Hédelin, Abbé d'Aubignac under the encouragement of Richelieu. The *Projet*, which argued against the immorality and profaneness of plays and players, summarized the ideological side of Richelieu's promotion of theater in France. In sum, the involvement of Richelieu in both the practice and theory of theater was all-encompassing, and, unsurprisingly, this literary facet was harshly criticized by his political opponents, who saw how the *cardinal-duc* used theater as a propaganda tool for strengthening his power.

No other early modern European royal favorite was as involved in dramatic poetry as Richelieu. Nevertheless, the situation of French theater under his government resonates with what had taken place some decades earlier in Spain and England, when the politics of these two kingdoms were dominated by the figures of court favorites. In the case of England, theatrical production began to thrive in London during the second half of the sixteenth century with the determinant incentive of the aristocracy, who gave patronage to playing companies.[14] One of the first companies to gain foothold in the capital, the Earl of Leicester's Man, was known, as was usual back then, by the name of his patron. At a time when players were defenseless before the City authorities, Leicester, a favorite of Queen Elizabeth, protected his company against hostility toward professional playing,[15] and his active role in this matter contributed positively to the establishment of other companies and the construction of purpose-built playhouses around London (Gurr, *The Shakespearian* 185–92). This support of theater, which Leicester used to advertise his power (White), was later continued by other favorite ministers, although after 1603, when King James I and his family gave royal patronage to the playing companies, the weight carried by the nobility in the advancement of English drama was somewhat eclipsed. During the Jacobean era, the engagement of the king's favorites with theater consisted mainly of the sponsorship of private performances. For instance,

Robert Cecil, whose short term as James' favorite was in many ways comparable to that of Lerma, Olivares, or Richelieu, entertained the royal family by organizing costly court spectacles (Croft). These events included dramatic performances, especially masques, and provided an opportunity for the promotion of playwrights, who were rewarded for their service, and their work received official recognition. Among these favored playwrights, Ben Jonson was the most successful poet of the early Stuart court and was often commissioned by the royal favorites, including the Duke of Buckingham, who appointed him to the office of Master of the Revels (Evans; Butler).

In Spain, the connection between royal favoritism and the expansion of theater is still clearer than in England. In this case, the role played by the Duke of Lerma, although more modest, reminds one of that of Cardinal Richelieu.[16] Lerma lacked the skills to write dramatic poetry, but he ignored and silenced the voices that were against the practice of theater and banned it in the late 1590s; thus his rise to power and abundant patronage had a direct and immediate impact on the blooming of drama in Spain (Búrdalo 177–9).[17] In the private sphere of the royal palace, plays were staged even before theater was officially permitted. In April 1599, seven months after the death of Philip II, the new king Philip III celebrated his wedding with Margaret of Austria in a sumptuous ceremony in Valencia, and not in Barcelona, as his father had prescribed, which was meticulously organized by Lerma (Williams 169–76). In the weeks prior to the arrival of the new queen from Graz to Valencia, the mourning of the deceased Philip II came to an end, and Philip III and Lerma together publicly enjoyed dancing, a common skill among European court favorites (Vega, *Fiestas de Denia* 213–5). Theater was also an entertainment for the courtiers gathered in Valencia in the weeks prior to the Queen's arrival to the city. From then until the end of his mandate, in 1618, the Duke of Lerma sponsored many other events involving dramatic performances. Throughout this time, new private theatrical spaces, such as the Casa del Tesoro in Madrid, were created, and the patios, balconies, and gardens of Lerma's palaces and estates were continuously adapted to stage elaborate performances. He used those spaces, as studied by Bernardo José García, to provide splendid court spectacles, by hiring the best actors, poets, and musicians of the day. The interest and power of the favorite were such that sometimes these artists were even absolved of their crimes and acquitted of various charges, in order to perform for the Duke.

This path of Lerma's theatrical patronage can be illustrated through the careers of Lope de Vega and Luis Vélez de Guevara. Lope was invited to the royal wedding festivities and composed an *auto sacramental* – *Las bodas entre el Alma y el Amor divino*, which allegorically exalted the king's favorite (Feros, *Duque de Lerma* 193–4) – that was staged during the celebrations of 1599 in Valencia.[18] From then, he was often under the service of Lerma and members of the favorite's clientele and wrote many dramas commissioned by them. The splendid properties of Lerma, where some of those dramas were performed, served, in turn, as the setting for the action of numerous plays by Lope (Wright; Arata). For his part, Vélez de Guevara, also an attendee at the 1599 marriage in Valencia and a prolific author of dramas on favorites, enjoyed a successful career as a playwright under the shadow of Lerma (Peale, "Three Power Plays"), which he continued to enjoy under the subsequent royal favorite, the Count-Duke of Olivares. Guevara's main patron and Lerma's son, the Count of Saldaña, was a poet himself, albeit rather substandard, who hosted a literary academy comprising Lope, Quevedo, and Cervantes, among others.

In sum, royal favorites knew the importance of theater as propaganda and used dramatic poetry for their own political purposes. Their personal patronage, which was more private in the case of Lerma and some English chief ministers and was more publicly institutionalized in the case of Richelieu, represented a great movement toward the development of theater in Western Europe.

Aside from the personal involvement of favorite ministers in theater, another aspect of the relationship between favoritism and theater was the situation of playwrights at courts dominated by royal favorites. Early modern courts were the center of patronage relationships, and in the age of royal favorites, these acted as the greatest patrons. Reaching the association with, and the patronage of, the king's favorite was the ultimate goal of any courtier and, naturally, of the playwrights who, attracted by the flow of wealth and honors circulating at court, were there to seek protection and status. This aim can be seen throughout the numerous plays that were dedicated to the favorites. Cardinal Richelieu, for example, appeared as the dedicatee of approximately twenty plays in the last ten years of his life (Howarth, "Mécénat et raison d'État" 63). Nevertheless, attracting the attention of a favorite was almost out of reach for most of the dramatists,[19] leaving them with little options other than to forge relationships with some of his many agents and subordinates. In those cases, the possibilities in succeeding in court increased depending on the proximity of the playwrights' patrons to the favorite: the closer to the favorite a patron was, the more beneficial for the playwright who served him. From this perspective, one may think that the dedications and petitions directly addressed to the favorites were rare compared to the many others that the favorite's relatives and clients received continually. In this epoch, in many parts of Europe, potential patrons had more petitioners than they could actually acknowledge, let alone satisfy (Harrison 52–3; Tropé, "Valimiento y mecenazgo" 132–3 and 154). These petitioners could apply, of course, to different patrons at the same time and doing so increase their likelihood to find one. An example of this mode of proceeding can be found in the multiple letters written by the historian Pedro Salazar de Mendoza in 1603 (*Cartas*), with the aim of finding funding for publishing his works, in only two days, to the Duke of Lerma and many of his supporters, including Pedro Franqueza and his son Valerio, Rodrigo Calderón, the Duke of Medinaceli, and the Count of Lemos. In this regard, Linda Peck comments on the forms or templates circulating in England and that clients used as models to write their petitions (*Court Patronage* 15–16).

In this context, dramatic writing became a strategy to penetrate the networks of influence and a gainful activity inserted into court politics. For playwrights of a court society, plays were cultural products susceptible to being exchanged for gifts, pensions, offices, titles, honors, and, in short, social status. Achieving these goals was of great importance, if not the writers' prime concern.[20] It must be said, however, that the guarantees of success for the literary aspirants were zero, and, more often than not, a mere acknowledgment of his work by a nobleman was a true accomplishment. The lack of generosity of those who sponsored the poets was a common complaint among the latter, and even a celebrated playwright like Lope de Vega, who served the crème de la crème of the Spanish nobility, spent his life seeking a source of regular income and lamented that: "The same way Nature created lame, one-eyed or hunchbacked men, it also created poor men, unfortunate men and poets, that in Spain are like prostitutes: everybody would lie down with them for a cheap price but, after leaving the brothel, they call them whores" (*Epistolario* 4:55).[21]

The types of gifts that were exchanged in the relationships of patronage varied and could include items as trivial as a pair of gloves (Peck, *Court Patronage* 19; Sieber, "Magnificent Fountain" 89–90), although, at least in Spain, the trade of "gloves" was commonly used as euphemism to express cash payment. A more desirable reward, at any rate, was to be appointed to a public administrative office or to be taken into the household of a nobleman. This objective was achieved by a considerable number of writers, and some of them, thanks to their enviable position, acted even as conduits to their own clients. This was the case of Antonio Hurtado de Mendoza, who, along with his friend Vélez de Guevara, belonged to the Count of Saldaña's household. In a poem, we can see Hurtado de Mendoza acting as a broker as he reminds a client of the "money for gloves" that is due to him for providing certain information in relation to the application for membership of a military order (Davies 36). This example illustrates the structure of a network based on patronage relationships and the circulation of favors within it. On the top of the chain is the king, whose special relationship with the Duke of Lerma allows the latter to channel the royal bounty toward his son the Count of Saldaña, who, in turn, uses those resources to sponsor literary activities and contract the permanent service of writers such as Vélez de Guevara and Hurtado de Mendoza. These playwrights not only benefit from the support given by their patron but, as seen in the case of Hurtado de Mendoza, they could also take advantage of their privileged position to create new sources of income.

It should not be surprising that a playwright, even one who is comparatively successful, is constantly seeking new sources of income. In the early modern age, writing was not a profession in the modern sense and playwrights could not rely solely on the benefits resulting from patronage, which were uncertain and inconstant. Being that these earnings were often insufficient, dramatists still depended on the sale of their plays to either playing companies or publishers as a source of quick money. In this period, only playwrights of great renown, such as Lope de Vega (García Reidy) and Ben Jonson (Ioppolo), seem to have secured some financial reward from publishing their works. For the most part, selling plays for public performance was the most common source of income for playwrights (Leavitt; Lough, "The Earnings" and "Drama and Society" 257). This staging purpose led dramatists to produce plays having in mind the audiences of commercial theaters, which included, in Spain, France, and England, a wide segment of the urban population, both male and female, ranging from thieves, servants, soldiers, students, and artisans to clerics, gentlemen, royal favorites, and monarchs.[22]

To stress the variety of spectators, one may first think of the areas where the playhouses were located. In London, some of the commercial theaters – such as the Globe and the Rose – were built in the borough of Southwark alongside prisons, taverns, gambling houses, and brothels (McDonald 226–7). The theatrical activity was immersed in this riotous atmosphere and Ben Jonson, for instance, was accused of murdering a fellow player (Wickham et al. 281). The playhouses in Madrid were surrounded by a milieu comparable to that of London (Fernández). Civic disorder and crimes were also frequent in Paris theaters, and sometimes the main protagonists of the disturbances were noblemen armed with swords and pistols. On this side of the social spectrum, some nobles in both Madrid and Paris confronted a similar ambiguity: they were eager to attend public performances but reluctant to pay for their special seats or for entrance to the theater (Varey and Shergold 1: 26; Howarth, *French Theatre* esp. 122–3 and 244). The Duke of Lerma and his closest creatures, such as Rodrigo Calderón, had private boxes in the *corrales* of Príncipe and Cruz, and so did King Philip IV, who in the Corral de la Cruz watched one of his mistresses acting (Albrecht 61–2; Fernández 73–4). English royal favorites also attended commercial theaters and, aimed by political intentions, arranged the performance of certain plays in public playhouses. This was the case of Shakespeare's drama concerning favorites, *Richard II*, which fascinated Robert Cecil, Walter Raleigh, and the Earl of Essex. The Duke of Buckingham arranged in 1628 the performance at the Globe of *Henry VIII*, also by Shakespeare, and left the playhouse in the middle of the play to show publicly, according to Hammer, his disconnection with the negative portrayal of the favorite character of the play (Hammer 33).

Dramas on favorites, therefore, were not only commissioned by and performed before select great lords and patrons on private households to celebrate the figure of a particular favorite or the institution of favoritism itself, but they were also presented to the heterogeneous audiences who attended commercial theaters and were not indifferent to the intrigues of the palace. In the playhouses, dramas featuring favorites satisfied a social interest in current politics, commented on the topic of favoritism, and certainly entertained playgoers with a theme that remained popular for decades.

Due to this wide interest in the topic of favoritism among socially diverse audiences, there was little distinction between theater intended for a commercial playhouse and for an aristocratic household, and plays were conveniently adjusted to public and private stages (Westfall; Trambaioli, "Lope de Vega" 38–9 and "Aquí, Senado, se acaba" 186–93). The three plays that are here examined in depth – *La paciencia en la fortuna*, *Le Favori, ou la Coquette*, and *Sejanus His Fall* – show that versatility of theatrical performances. The available sources register performances of those three plays in public theaters as well as a *mise en scène* of *Le Favori, ou la Coquette* in the gardens of Versailles; and there are clues that suggest that both *La paciencia en la fortuna* (Gómez, "La paciencia") and *Sejanus His Fall* (Cadman 1–22) were also presented at private events.

Past and present

When theater audiences viewed a favorite minister on stage, the action of the play being performed was set in a distant time and possibly place as well, and yet, playgoers, as the aforementioned performance of *Henry VIII* at the Globe suggests, recognized in the dramatic character the favorites of their own time. Indeed, the vast majority, if not all, of dramas on favorites had a historical and sometimes also a foreign setting, even as dramatists made clear references to the contemporary scene that the audiences were prompt to discern. Several reasons explain this paradox between past and present in the theatrical representations of favorite ministers.[23]

First, no early modern playwright could dramatize the life of a current royal favorite because dramatic censorship prohibited the *mise en scène* of living people of elevated status and contemporary events that could raise public controversy (Feros, "Historia y poesía" 15). Therefore, dramatists who intended to comment on current events and public figures, such as royal favoritism and its agents, were forced to cover their stories with historical settings. In other words, dramas concerning favorites had to feature characters and events from the past that were to a certain extent familiar to the audience. When dramas on favorites did not adhere to this guideline, instead of a historical setting, those plays were set in a distant land and an imaginary scenario with no apparent relation to the present surrounding the author, such as Alarcón's *El dueño de las estrellas* (c.1620–23), set in the kingdom of Crete, *The Queen of Corinth* (1616–17) by Fletcher, Field, and Massinger, set also in ancient Greece, or Desjardins' *Le Favori, ou la Coquette* (1664), set in the kingdom of Barcelona.

As an exception to this rule regarding the staging of non-contemporary royal favorites, Lerma might have been explicitly personified, as the protagonist of *The Spanish Duke of Lerma* (c. 1623), while he was still alive. Nevertheless, the original version of this play is now lost and what remains is a reworking of it by Robert Howard, *The Great Favourite* (1668). Moreover, the exact date of the original play is uncertain, and given that Lerma died in 1625, the text might have been written soon after his death, not to mention that Lerma was removed from power in 1618 and this play, in any case, was written in England and not in Spain. Further, it is highly possible, as Margaret Shewring suggests in her well-documented edition of the play, that *The Spanish Duke of Lerma* experienced some problems with censorship, which would explain why the play, readapted, did not appear until decades later. Similar circumstances seem to have experienced the anonymous drama concerning favorites *The Faithful Friends* (1620s), set in ancient Rome, which ironically and by all means anachronistically compared the favorites of Alexander the Great and Philip III: "Alexander the great had his Ephestion / Philip of Spaine his Lerma, not to offend" (145–6). Although there is no indication suggesting the intervention of official censorship, the unique surviving manuscript of *The Faithful Friends*, published by the Malone Society, shows marks left by contemporary correctors who made alterations and cuttings in the original text, especially in the controversial folio 4b that includes references to favorites and particularly the aforementioned line regarding Lerma, which was finally deleted. "Most of the cuts," Pinciss notes in the introduction, "seem to have been motivated by a wish to tone down the play's many references to potentially objectionable political topics" (xiii).

These two English plays concerned with favoritism and more specifically with the figure of Lerma were probably written as part of a widespread anti-Catholic tradition in England that, in the early 1620s, opposed the foreign policy of James I and his all-powerful minister the Duke of Buckingham, who in 1623 traveled to Madrid incognito to arrange the marriage, never consummated, between the Prince Charles of England and the Infanta Maria Anna of Spain (Redworth). The result of these marriage negotiations, known as the Spanish Match, was a debacle subsequently lampooned in the theater, as shown in Thomas Middleton's successful *A Game at Chess* (1624), which pointed satirically to the current relations between the English and Spanish monarchies under the framework of a game of chess (Fuchs 55–78).

A Game at Chess was an allegorical drama with no personal names but titles such as "White Duke" and "Black Duke," representing Buckingham and Olivares, respectively, and yet, the play was suppressed and its author imprisoned. This and the earlier examples serve to show that cloaking political commentaries under historical or allegorical frameworks was indeed insufficient to avoid censorship. In fact, it seems that most English dramatists who discussed political favoritism in their apparent history plays, except for Shakespeare, had problems with the authorities.[24] Likewise in Spain, Tirso de Molina, according to Albrecht, was banned from Madrid and the theater in 1625 due to the criticism of his dramas against favorite ministers (127–67).

Censors condemned a fair number of dramas on favorites because they thought, with good reasons, that those plays were not only dramatizing events from the past but also discussing important and controversial issues of the present. Censors, obviously, were not the only ones aware of this disguise. In fact, as McKendrick suggests, seventeenth-century audiences would hardly have a sound notion of history and therefore they would not be interested in the accuracy of past's representations (*Playing* 101). The explicit mention of a living royal favorite in a drama was not only censured and abnormal, as we have seen, but also unnecessary since most playgoers would view the character of any historical favorite only within their own contemporary frame of reference. In sum, the political immediacy of history dramas on favorites was a given.

Consequently, censorship is inadequate to fully understand the relationship between past and present that is characteristic of dramas on favorites. By setting these dramas in a distant past, playwrights are not just attempting to elude the censorial control, which, in any case, assumes that history plays talk about the present. Such a displacement is also due to the opportunities that history offers to dramatists, who explore the past as a source of exempla for dramatic purposes. When taking into consideration the figure of a favorite minister from the past, dramatists dispense with historiographical accuracy and focus on the "poetic truth" embedded in their plays.[25] In principle, these dramatic purposes are fairly distinguishable from those of the historical writing, although this distinction becomes less clear when we think of the rhetorical approach to history of the early modern *ars historica* (Grafton, *What Was History?*).[26] This approach is shared by contemporary artists of drama as well, many of whom developed their dramatic work side by side with historians. For example, Lope de Vega not only found material for his plays in the works of historians such as Florián de Ocampo and Juan de Mariana, but he also attempted in different ways to become a royal chronicler (Bershas). Lope failed to achieve this position, but Jean Racine, whose early education was shaped by the reading of Tacitus, was appointed as historiographer of King Louis XIV (Ranum, *Artisans* 278–332). Ben Jonson had also a close relationship with historians and his dramatic work, more notably *Sejanus His Fall*, shared the historiographical and political views of his time, especially the Tacitean ideas promoted by the Earl of Essex's circle (Worden, "Ben Jonson among the Historians"). Contrary to what these examples may suggest, that dramatists are influenced by historians, one may think of the protagonists of Pierre Corneille's and Jean de Rotrou's plays. These powerful images of chivalric knights became so popular that French official historians were forced to portray their kings in a similar way to the heroes that appeared on stage (Ranum, *Artisans* 118–9). Dramatic and historical writing, therefore, complemented each other and shared ideas in a mutual relationship.

This connection between dramatic and historical writing invites us to think on the general ideas that during the age of royal favoritism were common to both dramatists and historians. In this regard, if there is an intellectual framework to which the emergence of the political favoritism theme and consequently the development of dramas on favorites can be associated, that is undoubtedly the so-called Neostoicism.

Neostoicism

Stoicism spread in the late sixteenth and early seventeenth centuries in Europe through the works, mainly, of the Flemish humanist Justus Lipsius (1547–606), who succeeded in harmonizing the pagan Stoic philosophy with Christianity, thus originating the Neostoic movement. More importantly, Lipsius promoted the works of classical authors, and thanks to him, Stoicism through Seneca was blended with a pragmatic approach to history and politics through Tacitus. This combination was the true essence and novelty of the Neostoic or "Lipsian paradigm," which had an extraordinary impact on early modern European thought.[27]

While Senecan Stoicism, with its stress on the values of constancy and patience, had a long tradition continued by humanists such as Erasmus of Rotterdam in the first half of the sixteenth century, the legacy of Tacitus was practically inexistent. Up to the last quarter of the sixteenth century, Tacitus' popularity had never been comparable to that of other Roman thinkers and historians such as Cicero or Livy, who were the main references for classicists (Salmon, "Cicero," and Whitfield). This relative lack of recognition was to a certain extent due to Tacitus' rebukes to Christians, which tarnished his reputation lastingly. This obstacle diminished during the wars of religion that throughout the sixteenth century divided Europe between Catholics and Protestants and especially after the Catholic Church condemned Machiavelli in 1559. Henceforth, Tacitism offered "all the practical advantages associated with the teachings of Machiavelli without the obloquy attached to his name."[28] The popularity of Tacitus thus rose exponentially and more than one hundred editions of his *Annals* and *Histories* and a similar number of commentators of his works made him the most influential Roman historian in Europe during the first half of the seventeenth century (Burke). Largely responsible for this extensive popularity was Justus Lipsius.

Lipsius, who traveled around Europe and converted to Lutheranism and Calvinism before reconverting to Catholicism, had the ability to disseminate Tacitism, in its connection with Stoicism, among both Catholic and Protestant areas. His editions of Roman writers, including those of Seneca and Tacitus, and his philosophical and political treatises in Latin were followed by multiple translations into vernacular languages. His influence was thus heavily felt in Italy, Spain, France, Germany, and England, where his works served as lessons on political behavior to statesmen and particularly to favorite ministers.[29] Based on Lipsius' earlier translation, in 1614 Baltasar Álamos de Barrientos published his *Tácito Español Ilustrado con Aforismos* and dedicated it to Lerma. Nonetheless, Lerma had already been introduced to Lipsius through the advice of Antonio Pérez and Barrientos in the 1590s (Feros, *Duque de Lerma*; Pérez). Antonio Pérez went into exile and formed part, along with Ben Jonson, of the circle of the Earl of Essex, from where the cult of Lipsius spread around England (Ungerer). In turn, both Olivares' and Richelieu's statecrafts were shaped by the reading of Lipsius (Elliott, *Richelieu and Olivares*, 24–7).

The influence of Lipsius' Neostoicism, certainly, was determinant for the emergence of the early modern discourses on favoritism, which included political treatises and "mirrors of princes" but also historical and dramatic writing. By joining the ancient values of Stoicism to the cynical and unveiled view of politics provided by Tacitus, Lipsius created a particular outlook with a historical approach to early modern court life. Although Tacitus himself was not a philosopher, his research into the hidden motivations of power during the Roman early principate was loaded with moral judgments against the tyranny of emperors and their favorites. By means of the humanist trope *similitudo temporum* ("similar periods"), Lipsius insisted on the resemblances between the current political circumstances in Europe and Rome during the first century, thus viewing the *Annals* of Tacitus as "a theater of our modern life" (qtd. in Grafton, "Tacitus" 921).

One of the protagonists of Tacitus' account was precisely Seneca, whose service as an imperial advisor and tutor to Nero ended dramatically, according to Tacitus (Ker). This pagan portrait of Seneca was later blended with approaches to the Roman philosopher as a potential or secret Christian, and even Lipsius admitted a possible correspondence between Seneca and St. Paul (Blüher 259). The depiction of Seneca as a wise advisor and politician gained importance within the Neostoic movement, and in Spain, for many authors, Seneca became the positive model of the royal favorite (Blüher 488–507). In stark opposition, Sejanus, the imperial favorite of Tiberius, became a recurring image of the negative favorite and a popular name of opprobrium applied to contemporary royal favorites (Elliott, "Introduction" 2).[30]

These images of historical actors such as Seneca and Sejanus, and also medieval figures like Álvaro de Luna and Piers Gaveston, appealed strongly to the European societies that, during the sixteenth and seventeenth centuries, experienced the issues derived from the excessive power conferred to the monarchs' chief ministers. Staging historical favorites, as dramas on favorites characteristically did, was not an examination of events from the past but a way to explore and comment on contemporary royal favoritism.

Notes

1 Based on their titles, context, and some other information, such as summaries or mentions in contemporary records, we can deduce that some lost plays dealt with favoritism. This is the case of Lope's *La envidia y la privanza* that is mentioned in *El peregrino en su patria* (59), which could be the second part of Lope's *La fortuna merecida* (Restori 234), *La privanza desterrada*, and *La privanza del Rey don Emanuel* that Sommaia describes in his diary (174, 178, and 557), and the two-part play on Cardinal Wolsey (1601) (Matusiak 209).
2 Cauvin; Peale, "Comienzos" and "Los principios;" Campbell, "El poder."
3 Ferrer, "Lope de Vega y la dramatización de la materia genealógica (I)," "Lope de Vega y la dramatización de la materia genealógica (II)," "El juego del poder," and "Reyes y validos."
4 Among them Ana Isabel Sánchez in her prologue to Lope de Vega's *La fortuna merecida*, 615–22 and Wise 21–2. Javier González, in his introduction to Vélez de Guevara's *El Lucero de Castilla*, also regards the *dramas de privanza* as a subgroup within the genealogical drama and suggests subtle modifications to Ferrer's definition of those dramas (pp. 19–23). From a different point of view, Díez Borque (171–9) analyzes some of Lope's plays concerned with favoritism during the reign of Philip IV.
5 On the dramas on favorites by Damián Salucio del Poyo, which Ferrer briefly notes ("El juego del poder" 162–3), see Caparrós, *Entre validos y letrados*.
6 This last point is contextualized within a wider literary framework in Feros, "Images of Evil."
7 On the figure of the good favorite on the English stage, see Perry 55–94.
8 Other examples of Spanish plays portraying negative favorites are Montalbán's *El Mariscal de Birón* (Cauvin 414–23; MacCurdy 181–8), Lope's *La inocente sangre* (Wise 26–62) and *La quinta de Florencia* (Atienza). See also Herrero's study of the evil favorite in Calderón's theater.
9 All translations are mine except where otherwise noted. On the significance of those lines within the *El caballero de Olmedo*, see Profeti 116.
10 See especially Barton (105–19), who asserts that "*Volpone* was generated by *Sejanus*" (105), and Ayres (10).
11 Elliott, "Staying in Power" 118. On Lerma extensive patronage practice and liberality in permitting *mercedes*, as well as the resulting financial problems for the Spanish monarchy, see Feros, "Gobierno de Corte" 37, and *Duque de Lerma* 278–9. On Olivares' efforts to restrict the circulation of favors, see Elliott, *The Count-Duke of Olivares*, esp. 135–7.
12 On Lerma, see Feros, *Duque de Lerma* and *Gobierno de Corte*, and Alvar; on Buckingham, see the works by Levy Peck.
13 See especially Ranum, *Richelieu*, and the lucid study of patrons, brokers, and clients by Sharon Kettering.
14 According to Westfall, who studies the theater for aristocratic audiences in England, "virtually every known playwright (and probably most of those 'anons') occupied some position in one or more patronage network, so that to some extent we know that the great households patrons were fundamental to Renaissance public theater" (325).
15 This hostility stemmed fundamentally from the Puritan tradition in England, and from the Catholic Church in Spain and France (Lough, "Drama and Society" 241).
16 Although the terms of Olivares and Richelieu as chief ministers are contemporaneous, there are considerable differences between the two of them, for instance in regard to their involvement in theater. The comparative study of the two statesmen by John Elliot pays little attention to their dramatic activity,

but he mentions that Olivares' regime "took steps to prevent the publication of novels and plays" (*Richelieu and Olivares* 68). The article (González) that Elliott cites to make that claim shows that the animadversion of Castilian authorities, although not specifically Olivares, against theater was more profound and intended to ban commercial theaters, which culminated in their closing in the 1640s. Indeed, under the government of Olivares, court theater intensified to the detriment of public theaters (McKendrick, *Theatre* 209–37). This gradual decline of the *corrales* probably had significant consequences on the way in which favorite ministers were depicted in Spanish drama, because writing plays on monarchs and their ministers for an exclusive court audience would by some means constrain the scope of the playwrights. This circumstance might explain the appearance of court dramas featuring favorites like Francisco de Quevedo's *Cómo ha de ser el privado* (c. 1629), which has traditionally been considered an inflated panegyric to Olivares (Profeti 126–9), although its interpretation still remains ambivalent (Gilbert). Still more difficult to evaluate is the play, also attributed to Quevedo (Hernández 253–4), *La privanza desleal y voluntad por la fama*, which is preserved in the Biblioteca Nacional de España as a *suelta* and unlisted in the library's catalog.

17 Lerma's literary patronage and support of theater began during his term as viceroy of Valencia in 1595–1597 (Ferrer, "El duque de Lerma").

18 The auto was placed at the end of the second book of *El peregrino en su patria* (1604), 193–234.

19 Feros mentions two occasions in which, to petitioners, approaching the king first was a more convenient way to obtain favors from the highly solicited Duke of Lerma (*Gobierno de Corte* 38). This anomalous procedure is also mentioned by Rubens in a letter dated 1626 in which he compares Lerma to Richelieu (Schroth 4).

20 Juan Ruiz de Alarcón, who wrote several dramas on favorites in the late 1610s and early 1620s, ceased his literary activity once he achieved a secure position in the government administration and was protected by a relative of the king's favorite the Count-Duke of Olivares (Ferrer, "Teatro y mecenazgo" 115–8).

21 Translated by Carlos M. Gutiérrez, "The challenges of freedom: social reflexivity in the seventeenth-century literary field." *Hispanic Baroques: Reading Cultures in Context*, edited by N. Spadaccini and L. Martín-Estudillo, Vanderbilt UP, 2005, 153.

22 For the theater audiences in early modern Europe, see Lough, "Drama and Society," esp. 243–8; for Spain, France, and England, see McKendrick, *Theatre* 178–208; Albrecht 1–100; Lough, *Paris Theatre*; Howarth, *French Theatre* esp. 244–52; Gurr, *Playgoing*; Cerasano 195–9.

23 To my knowledge, in the only few cases in which early modern playwrights dramatized contemporary royal favorites, the latter had already passed away and governed in a country different to where the play was written such as the Dutch, Spanish, French, and Italian dramas that, from the 1620s, focused on the figure of the Earl of Essex, who died in 1601 (Hüsken; Smith). The first English play featuring Essex, *The Unhappy Favourite* (1682) by John Banks, was written later than its continental counterparts and received no influence from any of them. However, Essex had appeared briefly in an earlier English drama on favorite focused on the French Charles de Gontaut, Duc de Biron, who was executed in 1602: *The Conspiracy and Tragedy of Charles, Duke of Byron* (c. 1607), by George Chapman (Braunmuller 21–3). Both Chapman and Daniel, who wrote *The Tragedy of Philotas* (1604) alluding to Essex, run into trouble with the authorities; two other dramas containing Essex allusions were either withdrawn from performance or destroyed (Cain 52). For his part, Pierre Matthieu staged and depicted negatively his contemporary the Duke of

Épernon in *La Guisiade*; nevertheless, this play was not acted but only printed in 1589, the year that King Henri III was assassinated.

24 Worden ("Favourites" 171–2). Worden uses this circumstance to exclude Shakespeare from the list of English dramatists who dealt centrally with the theme of favoritism. Cf. MacFaul.

25 On theory of drama in Spanish Golden Age, see Wardropper, from whom I borrow the term "poetic truth" (213).

26 See, for instance, my study of Juan de Mariana, the most influential historian of early modern Spain (Gómez, *La creación*). The conclusions of that analysis can be summarized as follows: Juan de Mariana showed in many of his writings an extraordinary level of historiographical knowledge and criticism that, however, he disregarded when he wrote his *Historia general de España* (1592 in Latin and 1601 in Spanish), which was intended to convey the idea of a Spanish unity from ancient times by means of a deceitful narrative including, among other rhetorical devices, entirely invented speeches.

27 See the prologue of Adriana McCrea, who defines the "Lipsian Paradigm," for relevant bibliography concerning Neostoicism.

28 Elliott, *Richelieu and Olivares* 27. See also Benigno 22. For the "Tacitist Tradition," see the seminal work of Momigliano.

29 For details on the reception of Lipsius and Tacitus in Spain, England, and France, see Corbett, Salmon "Cicero" and "Stoicism," McCrea, and Amstutz, *La Fable du favori* 137–55.

30 Depictions of Senecan favorites can be seen in *La paciencia en la fortuna* and *Le Favori, ou la Coquette*, which are discussed in Chapters 2 and 3 of this book. The most renowned dramatic portrait of Sejanus, by Ben Jonson, is discussed in Chapter 4.

Works Cited

Albrecht, Jane. *The Playgoing Public of Madrid in the Time of Tirso de Molina*. New Orleans: UP of the South, 2001.

Alvar, Alfredo. *El Duque de Lerma: Corrupción y desmoralización en la España del siglo XVII*. Madrid: Esfera de los Libros, 2010.

Amstutz, Delphine. "Favoris et conseillers sur là scene tragique du premier XVIIe siècle." *Dramaturgies du conseil et de la délibération*, edited by Xavier Bonnier and Ariane Ferry, CÉRÉdI, Actes de colloques et journées d'étude, no. 16, 2016, pp. 1–9, accessed 20 March, 2020, http://ceredi.labos.univ-rouen.fr/public/?favoris-et-conseillers-sur-la.html

———. *La Fable du favori dans la littérature française du premier XVIIe siècle*. Dissertation, Université Paris-Sorbonne, 2013.

Arata, Stefano. "Proyección escenográfica de la Huerta del Duque de Lerma en Madrid." *Siglos dorados: homenaje a Agustín Redondo*, vol. 1, edited by P. Civil, Madrid, Castalia, 2004, pp. 33–52.

Arellano, Ignacio. *Los rostros del poder en el Siglo de Oro: Ingenio y espectáculo*. Renacimiento, 2011.

Atienza, Belén. "Arte y privanza en *La quinta de Florencia* de Lope de Vega: de los Médicis al duque de Lerma." *Bulletin of the Comediantes*, vol. 61, no. 2, 2009, pp. 1–18.

Aubignac, François Hédelin (Abbé d'). *La pratique du théâtre: oeuvre tres-necessaire a tous ceux qui veulent s'appliquer a la composition des poëmes dramatiques*, Antoine de Sommaville, 1657.

Ayres, Philip. "Introduction." *Sejanus His Fall*, by Ben Jonson, Manchester UP, 1990, pp. 1–44.

Banner, Lisa. *The Religious Patronage of the Duke of Lerma, 1598–1621*. Ashgate, 2009.

Barton, Anne. *Ben Jonson, Dramatist*. Cambridge UP, 1984.

Benigno, Francesco. *Favoriti e ribelli: Stili della politica baroca*. Bulzoni, 2011.

Bershas, Henry. "Lope de Vega and the Post of Royal Chronicler." *Hispanic Review*, vol. 31, no. 2, 1963, pp. 109–17.

Bevington, David, et al., editors. *The Cambridge Edition of the Works of Ben Jonson*. 7 vols., Cambridge UP, 2012.

Blüher, Karl. *Séneca en España: Investigaciones sobre la recepción de Séneca en España desde el siglo XIII hasta el siglo XVII*. 1969. Edited by Juan Conde, Gredos, 1983.

Bradner, Leicester. "The Theme of *privanza* in Spanish and English Drama 1590–1625." *Homenaje a William L. Fichter. Estudios sobre teatro antiguo hispánico y otros ensayos*, edited by A. David Kossoff and José Amor, Castalia, 1971, pp. 97–106.

Braunmuller, Albert. *Natural Fictions: George Chapman's Major Tragedies*. U of Delaware P, 1992.

Brown, Cedric, editor. *Patronage, Politics, and Literary Traditions in England, 1558–1658*. Wayne State UP, 1993.

Búrdalo, José Domínguez. "La inauguración del corral de comedias de Salamanca: una crónica sobre el auge escénico en la Castilla la Vieja de Felipe III (1603–1607)." *Bulletin of the Comediantes*, vol. 52 no. 1, 2000, pp. 171–219.

Burke, Peter. "A Survey of the Popularity of Ancient Historians, 1450–1700." *History and Theory*, vol. 5, no. 2, 1966, pp. 135–52.

Butler, Martin. "'We Are One Mans All': Jonson's *The Gipsies Metamorphosed*." Brown, 247–67.

Cadman, Daniel. *Sovereigns and Subjects in Early Modern Neo-Senecan Drama: Republicanism, Stoicism and Authority*. Ashgate, 2015.

Cain, Tom. "'Satyres, That Girde and Fart at the Time': *Poetaster* and the Essex Rebellion." *Refashioning Ben Jonson: Gender, Politics, and the Jonsonian Canon*, edited by J. Sanders et al., St. Martin's Press, 1998, pp. 48–70.

Campbell, Ysla. "El poder y la privanza: las propuestas de Alarcón." *eHumanista*, vol. 32, 2016, pp. 201–19.

Caparrós, Luis. *Entre validos y letrados: La obra dramática de Damián Salucio del Poyo*. Universidad de Valladolid, 1987.

———. "Privado." *Diccionario de la comedia del Siglo de Oro*, edited by Frank Casa et al., Castalia, 2001, pp. 240–2.

Cauvin, Mary Austin. *The comedia de privanza in the Seventeenth Century*. Dissertation, U of Pennsylvania, 1957.

Cerasano, Susan. "Performance: Audiences, Actors, and Stage Business." Kinney and Hopper, pp. 195–210.

Contarini, Simon. "Relación que hizo a la República de Venecia Simon Contarini de la embaxada que hizo a España y de todo lo que entendió de las cosas de ella, año de 1605." Appendix to L. Cabrera de Córdoba, *Relaciones de las cosas sucedidas en la corte de España desde 1599 hasta 1614*, J. Martín Alegría, 1857, pp. 563–83.

Corbett, Theodore. "The Cult of Lipsius: A Leading Source of Early Modern Spanish Statecraft." *Journal of the History of Ideas*, vol. 36, no. 1, 1975, pp. 139–52.

Couton, Georges. *Richelieu et le théâtre*. 1986. Eurédit, 2008.

Crivellari, Daniele. "Intrigo a palazzo: la tematica del conflitto nelle *comedias de privanza* di Luis Vélez de Guevara." *Escritura y conflicto / Scrittura e conflitto*, vol. 1, edited by A. Cancellier et al., ASIPI Instituto Cervantes, 2006, pp. 103–14.

Croft, Pauline. "Can a Bureaucrat Be a Favourite? Robert Cecil and the Strategies of Power." Elliott and Brockliss, pp. 81–95.

Davies, Gareth. *A Poet at Court: Antonio Hurtado de Mendoza, 1586–1644*. Dolphin, 1971.

Desjardins, Marie-Catherine (Madame de Villedieu). *Le Favori*. Edited by Delphine Amstutz, Hermann, 2017.

Díez Borque, José María. *Sociología de la comedia española del siglo XVII*. Cátedra, 1976.

El burlador de Sevilla (attributed to Tirso de Molina). 18th ed. Edited by A. Rodríguez, Cátedra, 2010.

Elias, Norbert. *La sociedad cortesana*. 1969. 2nd ed. Fondo de Cultura Económica, 2012.

Elliott, John. *Richelieu and Olivares*. Cambridge UP, 1984.

———. "Introduction." Elliott and Brockliss, pp. 1–10.

———. "Staying in Power: The Count Duke of Olivares." Elliott and Brockliss, pp. 112–22.

———. *The Count-Duke of Olivares: The Statesman in an Age of Decline*. Yale UP, 1986.

Elliott, John, and Laurence Brockliss, editors. *The World of the Favourite*. Yale UP, 1999.

Evans, Robert. *Ben Jonson and the Poetics of Patronage*. Bucknell UP, 1989.

Fernández, Esther. "Los corrales de comedias del siglo XVII madrileño: espacios de sensualidad urbana." *Bulletin of the Comediantes*, vol. 60, no. 1, 2008, pp. 71–90.

Fernández Mosquera, Santiago. "Quevedo y el valimiento: del *Discurso de las privanzas* hasta *Cómo ha de ser el privado*." *Bulletin of Spanish Studies*, vol. 90, no. 4–5, 2013, pp. 551–76.

Feros, Antonio. *El Duque de Lerma: Realeza y privanza en la España de Felipe III*. Marcial Pons, 2002.

———. *Gobierno de Corte y Patronazgo Real en el Reinado de Felipe III (1598–1621)*. Thesis, Universidad Autónoma de Madrid, 1986.

———. "Historia y poesía: monarcas y favoritos en las obras de Marlowe y Mira de Amescua." *Del poder y sus críticos en el mundo ibérico del Siglo de Oro*, edited by I. Arellano et al., Iberoamericana-Vervuert, 2013, pp. 111–42.

———. "Images of Evil, Images of Kings: The Contrasting Faces of the Royal Favourite and the Prime Minister in Early Modern European Political Literature, *c.* 1570–*c.* 1650," Elliott and Brockliss, pp. 205–22.

Ferrer Valls, Teresa. "El duque de Lerma y la corte virreinal en Valencia: fiestas, literatura y promoción social. *El prado de Valencia* de Gaspar Mercader." *Quaderns de filologia. Estudis literaris*, vol. 5, 2000, pp. 257–72.

———. "El juego del poder: Lope de Vega y los dramas de la privanza." *Modelos de vida en la España del Siglo de Oro*, vol. 1, edited by I. Arellano and M. Vitse, Iberoamericana, 2004, pp. 159–85.

———. "Lope de Vega y la dramatización de la materia genealógica (I)." *Cuadernos de Teatro Clásico*, vol. 10, 1998, pp. 215–31.

———. "Lope de Vega y la dramatización de la materia genealógica (II): lecturas de la historia." *La teatralización de la historia en el Siglo de Oro español: Actas del III coloquio del Aula-Biblioteca Mira de Amescua*, edited by R. Castilla and M. González, Universidad de Granada, 2001, pp. 13–51.

———. "Reyes y validos en los dramas genealógicos de Lope de Vega." *La voz de Clío: imágenes del poder en la comedia histórica del Siglo de Oro*, edited by Oana Andreia, Mariela Insúa, and Antonie Mihail. Editura Universitaria, 2012, pp. 133–45.

———. "Teatro y mecenazgo en el Siglo de Oro: Lope de Vega y el duque de Sessa." *Mecenazgo y humanidades en tiempos de Lastanosa. Homenaje a Domingo Ynduráin*, edited by A. Egido and J. E. Laplana, Institución Fernando el Católico, 2008, pp. 113–34.

Fuchs, Barbara. *The Poetics of Piracy: Emulating Spain in English Literature*. U of Pennsylvania P, 2013.

García García, Bernardo José. "Las fiestas de Corte en los espacios del valido: la privanza del Duque de Lerma." *La fiesta cortesana en la época de los Austrias*, edited by García and María Luisa Lobato, Junta de Castilla y León, 2003, pp. 35–77.

García Reidy, Alejandro. "From Stage to Page: Editorial History and Literary Promotion in Lope de Vega's *Partes de comedias*." *A Companion to Lope de Vega*, edited by A. Samson and J. Thacker, Tamesis, 2008, pp. 51–60.

Gilbert, Françoise. "*¿Cómo ha de ser el privado?*, o cómo el tiempo dramático modela el tiempo histórico." *Tiempo e historia en el teatro del Siglo de Oro*. Edited by I. Rouane and Philippe Meunier, Presses universitaires de Provence, 2015, pp. 223–31.

Gómez Martos, Francisco. *La creación de una historia nacional. Juan de Mariana y el papel de la Antigüedad en la Edad Moderna*. Instituto de Historiografía Julio Caro Baroja, 2018.

———. "*La paciencia en la fortuna*: An Unprinted Play by Lope de Vega." *Arte nuevo. Revista de estudios áureos*, vol. 6, 2019, pp. 57–89.

González, Ángel. "Quevedo, Tirso y las comedias ante la Junta de Reformación." *Boletín de la Real Academia Española*, vol. 25, 1946, pp. 43–84.

Grafton, Anthony. "Tacitus and Tacitism." *The Classical Tradition*, edited by A. Grafton et al., Harvard UP, 2010, pp. 920–4.

———. *What Was History? The Art of History in Early Modern Europe*. Cambridge UP, 2007.

Gurr, Andrew. *Playgoing in Shakespeare's London*. 2nd ed. Cambridge UP, 1996.

———. *The Shakespearian Playing Companies*. Clarendon P, 1996.

Halpern, Cynthia. *The Political Theater of Early Seventeenth-Century Spain, with Special Reference to Juan Ruiz de Alarcón*. Peter Lang, 1993.

Hammer, Paul. "Shakespeare's *Richard II*, the Play of 7 February 1601, and the Essex Rising." *Shakespeare Quarterly*, vol. 59, no. 1, 2008, pp. 1–35.

Harrison, George. *Elizabethan Plays and Players*. 1940. U of Michigan P, 1956.

Hernández, María. "Teatro inédito atribuido a Quevedo." *Compostella Aurea: Actas del VIII Congreso de la AISO*, edited by A. Azaústre and Santiago Fernández, Universidade de Santiago de Compostela, 2011, pp. 253–60.

Herrero, Javier. "The Devil as *Favorito* in Calderón's Theater." *«Por discreto y por amigo». Mélanges offerts Aà Jean Canavaggio*, edited by Christophe Couderc and Benoît Pellistrandi, Casa de Velázquez, 2005, pp. 295–303.

Howarth, William D. "Mécénat et raison d'État: Richelieu, Corneille et la tragédie politique." *L'âge d'or du mécénat (1598–1661): Actes du colloque international CNRS*, edited by R. Mousnier and J. Mesnard, Éditions du Centre National de la Recherche Scientifique, 1985, pp. 59–68.

———, editor. *French Theatre in the Neo-classical Era, 1550–1789*. Cambridge UP, 1997.

Hüsken, Wim. "Queen Elizabeth and Essex: A Dutch Rethoricians' Play." *Leeds Studies in English*, vol. 32, 2001, 151–70.

Ioppolo, Grace. "The Transmission of an English Renaissance Play-Text." Kinney and Hopper, pp. 545–59.

Jonson, Ben. *Sejanus His Fall*. Edited by Tom Cain. Bevington et al., vol. 2, pp. 195–391.

———. *Volpone*. Edited by Richard Dutton. Bevington et al., vol. 3, pp. 1–191.

Keenan, Siobhan. "Representing the Duke of Buckingham: Libel, Counter-Libel and the Example of *The Emperor's Favourite*." *Literature Compass*, vol. 9, 2012, pp. 292–305.

Ker, James. "Seneca in Tacitus." *A Companion to Tacitus*, edited by V. E. Pagán, Wiley-Blackwell, 2012, pp. 305–29.

Kettering, Sharon. *Patrons, Brokers, and Clients in Seventeenth-Century France*. Oxford UP, 1986.

Kinney, Arthur, and Thomas Hopper, editors. *A New Companion to Renaissance Drama*. John Wiley and Sons Ltd., 2017.

La privanza desleal y voluntad por la fama. T-55293-21 (provisional catalog number). Biblioteca Nacional de España, Madrid. 46–67v.

Leavitt, Sturgis. "Spanish *Comedias* as Pot Boilers." *PMLA*, vol. 82, no. 2, 1967, pp. 178–84.

Lough, John. "Drama and Society." *The New Cambridge Modern History*, vol. 4, edited by J. P. Cooper, Cambridge UP, 1970, pp. 239–59.

———. *Paris Theatre Audiences in the Seventeenth & Eighteenth Centuries*. Oxford UP, 1957.

———. "The Earnings of Playwrights in Seventeenth-Century France." *The Modern Language Review*, vol. 42, no. 3, 1947, pp. 321–36.

MacCurdy, Raymond. *The Tragic Fall: Don Álvaro de Luna and Other Favorites in Spanish Golden Age Drama*. U of North Carolina P, 1978.

MacFaul, Tom. "'A Kingdom with My Friend': Favorites in Shakespeare." *Literary Milieux: Essays in Text and Context Presented to Howard Erskine-Hill*. Edited by D. Womersley and R. McCabe, U of Delaware P, 2008, pp. 52–71.

Marlowe, Christopher. *Edward II*. Rev. edition by Martin Wiggins and Robert Lindsey, Bloomsbury, 2014.

Matusiak, Christopher. "Lost Stage Friars and their Narratives." *Lost Plays in Shakespeare's England*. Edited by D. McInnis and M. Steggle, Palgrave Macmillan, 2014, pp. 208–28.

McCrea, Adriana. *Constant Minds: Political Virtue and the Lipsian Paradigm in England, 1584–1650*. U of Toronto P, 1997.

McDonald, Russ. *The Bedford Companion to Shakespeare: An Introduction with Documents*. Bedford Books of St. Martin's P, 1996.

McKendrick, Melveena. *Playing the King: Lope de Vega and the Limits of Conformity*. Woodbridge, Tamesis, 2000.

———. *Theatre in Spain: 1490–1700*. Cambridge UP, 1989.

Mesnard, Jean. "Richelieu et le théâtre." *Richelieu et le monde de l'esprit*, edited by the Chancellerie des Universités de Paris et Académie Française, Imprimerie Nationale, 1985, pp. 193–206.

Middleton, Thomas. *A Game at Chess*. *Thomas Middleton: The Collected Works*. Edited by Gary Taylor and John Lavagnino, Oxford UP, 2007, pp. 1773–1885.

Mira de Amescua, Antonio. *La confusión de Hungría*. Edited by C. Argente. *Teatro completo*. Vol. 5, edited by A. de la Granja, Universidad de Granada, 2005, pp. 153–261.

Momigliano, Arnaldo. "Tacitus and the Tacitist Tradition." *Tacitus*, edited by Rhiannon Ash, Oxford UP, 2012, pp. 411–34.

Morgan, Victor. "Su alcune forme di padrinaggio nell'Inghilterra dei secoli XVI e XVII." *Padrini e clienti nell'Europa moderna (secoli XV-XIX)*, edited by A. Maczak and M. A. Romani, Astrea, 1986, pp. 23–45.

Peale, C. George. "Comienzos, enfoques y constitución de la comedia de privanza en la *Tercera parte de las comedias de Lope de Vega y otros auctores*." *Hispanic Review*, vol. 72, no. 1, 2004, pp. 125–56.

———. "Los principios de la comedia de privanza y la vuelta genérica de Ruiz de Alarcón. Nuevos bocetos y nuevas directrices." *Alarconiana IV: Estudios sobre la obra de Juan Ruiz de Alarcón*, edited by Ysla Campbell and Édgar García, Universidad Autónoma de Ciudad Juárez, 2017, pp. 11–36.

———. "Three Power Plays for the Duke of Lerma by Luis Vélez de Guevara." *Arte nuevo. Revista de estudios áureos*, vol. 7, 2020, pp. 102–134.

Peck, Linda. *Court Patronage and Corruption in Early Stuart England*. Unwin Hyman, 1990.

———. "Monopolizing Favour: Structures of Power in the Early Seventeenth-Century English Court." Elliott and Brockliss, pp. 54–70.

Pérez, Antonio. *Suma de preceptos justos, necesarios y provechosos en Consejo de Estado al Rey Felipe III, siendo Príncipe; Aforismos sacados de la Historia de Publio Cornelio Tácito*. Edited by Modesto Santos, Anthropos, 1991.

Pérez de Montalbán, Juan. *Amor, privanza y castigo. Primero tomo de las Comedias del Doctor Juan Pérez de Montalbán*. A. Vázquez, 1638.

Perry, Curtis. *Literature and Favoritism in Early Modern England*. Cambridge UP, 2006.

Profeti, María G. "Funciones teatrales y literarias del personaje del privado." Tropé, pp. 113–29.

Quevedo, Francisco de. *Cómo ha de ser el privado*. Edited by L. Gentilli, Mauro Baroni, 2004.

Ranum, Orest. *Artisans of Glory: Writers and Historical Thought in Seventeenth-Century France*. U of North Carolina P, 1980.

———. *Richelieu and the Councillors of Louis XIII: A Study of the Secretaries of State and Superintendents of Finance in the Ministry of Richelieu, 1635–1642*. Clarendon P, 1963.

Redworth, Glyn. *The Prince and the Infanta: The Cultural Politics of the Spanish Match*. Yale UP, 2003.

Restori, Antonio. "Obras de Lope de Vega - publicadas por la Real Academia Española." *Zeitschrift für romanische Philologie*, vol. 28, no. 2, 1904, pp. 231–56.

Sáez, Adrián. "De la privanza en Calderón: *Los cabellos de Absalón* y *La hija del aire*." *Bulletin of Spanish Studies*, vol. 92, no. 2, 2015, pp. 167–77.

Salazar de Mendoza, Pedro. *Cartas de Pedro Salazar de Mendoza con el envío de su crónica del cardenal Tavera*. Est. 198. Epsilon 32.3.4 (14). Biblioteca Estense-Universitaria, Modena. 121–129v.

Salmon, John. "Cicero and Tacitus in Sixteenth-Century France." *The American Historical Review*, vol. 85, no. 2, 1980, pp. 307–31.

———. "Stoicism and Roman Example: Seneca and Tacitus in Jacobean England." *Journal of the History of Ideas*, vol. 50, no. 2, 1989, pp. 199–225.

Salucio del Poyo, Damián. *La privanza y caída de don Álvaro de Luna. Comedias*, edited by Carmen Hernández, Academia Alfonso X el Sabio, 1985, pp. 239–376.

Schroth, Sarah. *The Private Picture Collection of the Duke of Lerma*. Dissertation, New York U, 1990.

Shakespeare, William. *Richard II*. Edited by A. Dawson and P. Yachnin, Oxford UP, 2011.

Shewring, Margaret. *A Critical Edition of Sir Robert Howard's* The Great Favourite; Or, The Duke of Lerma. Garland, 1988.

Sieber, Harry. "Cloaked History: Power and Politics in *La Estrella de Sevilla*." *Gestos: Teoría y práctica del teatro hispánico*, vol. 17, 1994, pp. 133–45.

———. "The Magnificent Fountain: Literary Patronage at the Court of Philip III." *Cervantes*, vol. 18, no. 2, 1998, pp. 85–116.

Smith, Winifred. "The Earl of Essex on the Stage." *PMLA*, vol. 39, no. 1, 1924, pp. 147–73.

Sommaia, Girolamo da. *Diario de un estudiante de Salamanca: La crónica inédita de Girlamo da Sommaia (1603–1607)*. Edited by George Haley, Universidad de Málaga, 2012.

Soria, Enrique. "La imagen del poder. Un acercamiento a las prácticas de visualización del poder en la España moderna." *Historia y Genealogía*, vol. 1, 2011, pp. 5–10.

Steggle, Matthew. *Digital Humanities and the Lost Drama of Early Modern England: Ten Case Studies*. Ashgate, 2015.

Tacitus, Cornelius. *The Annals*. Edited by J. Yardley and A. Barrett. Oxford UP, 2008.

The Emperor's Favourite. Edited by Siobhan Keenan, Manchester UP, 2010.

The Faithful Friends. Edited by G. M. Pinciss, Malone Society, 1975.

Trambaioli, Marcella. "'Aquí, Senado, se acaba...': normas implícitas y rasgos dramáticos del teatro de cámara de Lope de Vega." *Norme per lo spettacolo. Norme per lo spettatore*, edited by G. Poggi and M. G. Profeti, Alinea, 2011, pp. 185–98.

———. "Lope de Vega y la casa de Moncada." *Criticón*, vol. 106, 2009, pp. 5–44.

Tropé, Hélène. "Valimiento y mecenazgo. Los artistas y los escritores ante el Duque de Lerma, valido de Felipe III (1598–1621)." Tropé, pp. 131–80.

———, editor. *La représentation du favori dans l'Espagne de Philippe III et de Philippe IV*, Presses Sorbonne nouvelle, 2010.

Ungerer, Gustav. *A Spaniard in Elizabethan England: the Correspondence of Antonio Pérez's Exile*. 2 vols. Tamesis, 1974.

Varey, John, and Norman Shergold. *Teatros y comedias en Madrid: estudio y documentos*. 6 vols. Támesis, 1971.

Vega, Lope de. *El caballero de Olmedo. Fuente Ovejuna*. Edited by M. G. Profeti, Biblioteca Nueva, 2002.

———. *El duque de Viseo*. Edited by M. Calderón. *Comedias de Lope de Vega. Parte VI*. Vol. 2, edited by V. Pineda and G. Pontón, Milenio, 2005, pp. 1031–60.

———. *El peregrino en su patria*. Edited by Juan Bautista Avalle-Arce, Castalia, 1973.

———. *Epistolario de Lope de Vega Carpio*. 4 vols. Edited by Agustín González de Amezúa, Real Academia Española, 1935–1943.

———. *Fiestas de Denia*. Edited by M. G. Profeti and B. García García, Alinea, 2004.

———. *La fortuna merecida. Comedias. Parte XI*. Vol. 2. Edited by Ana Isabel Sánchez, Gredos, 2012, pp. 611–783.

Vélez de Guevara, Luis. *El Lucero de Castilla y Luna de Aragón*. Edited by William R. Manson and C. George Peale, introductions by Javier J. González Martínez and Gareth A. Davies, Juan de la Cuesta, 2013.

Wardropper, Bruce. "La comedia española del Siglo de Oro." *Teoría de la comedia*, by Elder Olson, Ariel, 1978, pp. 181–242.

Westfall, Suzanne. "'What Revels are in Hand?' Performances in the Great Households." Kinney and Hopper, pp. 322–36.

White, Paul. "Patronage, Protestantism, and Stage Propaganda in Early Elizabethan England." Brown, pp. 111–24.

Whitfield, John. "Livy > Tacitus." *Classical Influences on European Culture A.D. 1500–1700*, edited by R. Bolgar, Cambridge UP, 1976, pp. 281–93.

Wickham, Glynne, et al. *English Professional Theatre, 1530–1660*. Cambridge UP, 2000.

Williams, Patrick. "'Un estilo nuevo de grandeza.' El duque de Lerma y la vida cortesana en el reinado de Felipe III (1598–1621)." *Dramaturgia festiva y cultura nobiliaria en el siglo de oro*, edited by B. García and M. L. Lobato, Iberoamericana, 2007, pp. 169–202.

Wise, Carl. *Shadow of the King: Privanza and Perceptions of Royal Power in Seventeenth-Century Spanish Theater*. Dissertation, U of Georgia, 2011.

Worden, Blair. "Ben Jonson among the Historians." *Culture and Politics in Early Stuart England*, edited by K. Sharpe and P. Lake, Stanford UP, 1993, pp. 67–89.

———. "Favourites on the English Stage." Elliott and Brockliss, pp. 159–83.

Wright, Elizabeth. *Pilgrimage to Patronage: Lope de Vega and the Court of Philip III, 1598–1621*. Bucknell UP, 2001.

2 Favorites in Spanish drama

The business of theater that began to flourish in Spain in the last three decades of the sixteenth century was, to a certain extent, restrained by the conservative and austere personality of King Philip II and his circle of ecclesiastical counselors. The controversy about whether theater should be allowed in Spain reached its peak in the 1590s when a group of distinguished thinkers cried out against the practice of theater (Suárez). The pressure of these ideas and the premature death of the king's daughter, Catalina Micaela, Duchess of Savoy (1567–97), motivated Philip II to ban theatrical performances, first in Madrid (November 1597) and then in the group of kingdoms of the Spanish monarchy (May 1598). Meanwhile, Philip II had asked some of his closest advisors, among them García de Loaysa y Girón, their opinion on the matter. García de Loaysa, whose report against the performance of plays from 1598 is preserved in numerous manuscript copies, was preceptor of Prince Philip and part of the faction trying to persuade the King not to favor Francisco Gómez de Sandoval the Marquis of Denia and future Duke of Lerma, who had won the affection of the young Prince by means of adulation, presents, including money, and by accompanying him to hunt and play cards (Mrozek 62). In this sense, Loaysa and the Marquis of Denia were rivals at court and each one represented opposite views of how the future Philip III should reign (Centenera 73). Committed to Loaysa's cause was also the Jesuit historian Juan de Mariana, who was patronized and favored in court by Loaysa. Loaysa commissioned Mariana to write a political treatise, *De rege et regis institutione*, published in 1599, with the purpose of instructing the Prince. In this work, Mariana underlined the dangers that a king might face by sharing his sovereignty with a favorite minister or *privado*, and some passages of the text alluded to the Prince and the Marquis of Denia. The *De rege* was partially written in the mid-1590s, and toward 1598, when Philip II ordered the closure of public theaters and requested Loaysa's opinion, a chapter in opposition to theatrical representations was added to the book. In September of that same year, Philip II died, and immediately after, the new king Philip III made the Marquis of Denia his sole favorite. This political movement had momentous consequences in the Spanish court, given that the faction of the Marquis would henceforth overshadow any other group of power. As a result, many of the most influential ministers of Philip II and especially those who questioned Philip III's exceptional affection toward the Marquis were quickly removed from their positions and replaced by people associated with the new royal favorite. García de Loaysa, bitter enemy of theater, was one of the first to be demoted and died in 1599 because, Cabrera affirms, the King treated him with "disfavor" (10). Mariana, for his part, lost his greatest contact in court, and throughout the two decades that Lerma was the king's favorite, he suffered the censorship and persecution of the favorite's clan. His celebrated history of Spain was defamed by the authorities and submitted for alterations. Moreover, in 1609 Mariana was imprisoned due to the publication of a book in Latin, *Tractatus septem*, which included a new attack against theater (Gómez, *La creación*, esp. 43–51).

Following Philip II's death, the Duke of Lerma was *de facto* the person who took care of state affairs in the king's place. This concentration of political responsibilities on a single favorite minister contrasted to the regime based on the plurality of Councils that had characterized the structure of the Spanish government during most of the sixteenth century.[1] On the one hand, in order to institutionalize his position, Lerma became *de iure* a kind of prime minister, an intermediary between the monarch and the administration, by means of a royal decree (known as decree of signed delegation, 1612) in which Philip III stated that Lerma's signature had the same validity as his and ordered the councilors to obey the favorite's orders.[2] On the other hand, in order to dispel suspicions about his abuse of power, Lerma fomented a propaganda campaign whose objectives were both to emphasize the importance of the favorite minister in assisting the king and to portray himself not as a usurper but as a representative or *alter ego* of the monarch. This "Lermist" program included portraits (by Juan Pantoja and Rubens, among other artists) in which the favorite imitated the king's pose and carried the military insignia of the monarch (Schroth 5 and 11; Mrozek 85).[3]

Due to the structural changes that the new government of Philip III and his chief minister introduced from the beginning, it comes as no surprise that Philip II's decree from November 1597 prohibiting theatrical activities was in force only for a short period of time. From the first years of the seventeenth century, numerous playhouses or *corrales* were built around the entire Iberian Peninsula and performances at court multiplied. The documentation about when Spanish theaters reopened appears to be somewhat imprecise: Cabrera records this reopening twice, in April 1599 and in February 1600 (18, 59–60); Pellicer mentions the celebration of a meeting between counselors and theologians that was approved by the Duke of Lerma in April 1600 and that led to the permission of dramatic performances (109–12). In any case, regardless of the exact date and mode by which theater became permitted again, it seems clear that Lerma's government was in favor of the theatrical activity being resumed. In addition, the Duke and his close circle exercised a direct opposition to some of the most prominent defenders of the theater's illicitness, by excluding them from royal favor, as in the case of García de Loaysa, and even persecuting them, as in the case of Juan de Mariana. Beyond these circumstances, Lerma had a more important reason to promote theater: drama, like any other literary and artistic field in which Lerma involved himself, was used as a sometimes costly court entertainment, a public display of his wealth and status, and a propagandistic means in his permanent campaign to justify his position as the king's favorite.

Comedias de privanza

Lerma's rise to power and the appearance of dramas on favorites in Spain were simultaneous. Some of the earliest plays featuring favorites were due to Damián Salucio del Poyo, who in the first few years of the seventeenth century staged the rise and fall of Álvaro de Luna and Ruy López Dávalos.[4] These two Castilian constables had been literary subjects since the fifteenth century when contemporary poets such as Jorge Manrique and the first Marquis of Santillana addressed the issues related to their mighty positions in the court of King John II in relation to the inconstancy of fortune and the irrevocability of death. The protagonists of Salucio del Poyo's dramas are also favorites who experience the vicissitudes of fortune and, after being prosperous and favored by the king, fall inevitably in disgrace and, in the case of Álvaro de Luna, death. Nevertheless, the pyramidal structure of these plays in which fortune is the course of action had a long tradition in European literature and went back to classical works and, in the Middle Ages, to those of humanists such as Boccaccio and Petrarch, who preceded and influenced the poetry of Manrique and Santillana. For instance, Boccaccio's *De Casibus Virorum Illustrium* (c. 1360) included two-part stories on the ascent and descent of distinguished people who were subdued by the capricious fortune. This work in Latin was translated into multiple vernacular languages and inspired literary writings such as the *Canterbury Tales* and political treatises known as "mirror for magistrates or princes."[5] A similar popularity experienced the dialogues focused on the fluctuations of fortune included in Petrarch's *De remediis utriusque fortunae*, which was translated into Spanish and reprinted repeatedly in the sixteenth century as *De los remedios contra próspera y adversa Fortuna.*[6] Petrarch's treatise on fortune was divided into two books dealing with fortune's favors and disfavors in the first and the second book, respectively (Vaccari 51–2). This tradition about the *fortuna bifrons* weighed heavily on the development of dramas on favorites, particularly in Spain (Gutiérrez), where numerous plays relate the position of the royal favorite to the wheel of fortune and some of them are divided into two parts and include the *próspera* and *adversa fortuna* in their titles.[7]

Based on this emphasis on an unstable fortune that determines the destiny of royal favorites, scholars tend to perceive Salucio del Poyo's early plays on Álvaro de Luna and Ruy López Dávalos as prototypes for the rest of Spanish *comedias de privanza*,[8] or, more generally, to define dramas on favorites as plays focused on the rise and fall of power of favorite ministers and the issues that those changes prompt.[9] This perception and unadorned definition, however, appear somewhat misleading for several reasons. First, it must be noticed that a significant number of Spanish dramas on favorites exclude the fall of the protagonist, who, instead, at the end of the play is firmly established in his privileged position.[10] The author of *La privanza desleal y voluntad por la fama* (1620s), attributed to Quevedo, goes as far as to present a favorite who assumes control of the kingdom once the king is dethroned. The fact that numerous dramas on favorites present a fortunate ending for the protagonists, in turn, dismisses the hypothesis that this type of drama is by definition tragic, as some scholars suggested (MacCurdy).[11] Likewise, there are plays in which the rise of the favorites is omitted, thus beginning the stories of the favored ministers *in medias res*. Sometimes, these last plays end also without a fallen favorite, notably Guevara's *El conde don Pero Vélez y Sancho el Deseado*. A more singular case can be seen in *La paciencia en la fortuna*, in which an ex-favorite who lives retired in his own estates declines to be the favorite of the new young king and, after being imprisoned and subsequently pardoned, he is restored to his initial position.

In addition, although the notion of an unpredictable fortune is elemental in dramas on favorites, scholars tend to accentuate fortune's influence and philosophical dimensions over the favorite's autonomy and the political immediacy of those dramas.[12] George Peale reacted to this tendency by arguing that plays concerning favorites are not philosophical dramas and that the abstract notion of fortune would hardly be appealing to theater goers. Instead, Peale adds, the audience's high consciousness of the topic of favoritism was due to the current political events and, more precisely, to the sudden and meteoric rise to power of the Duke of Lerma ("Comienzos" 133–4).[13] To Peale's point of view, I would add some further considerations.

It is important to consider the historical context, and more specifically Lerma's years as chief minister, in order to understand not only the emergence and development but also some fundamental characteristics and concepts, including that of fortune, of dramas on favorites in Spain. To my knowledge, no one has suggested that plays such as *Cómo ha de usarse del bien y ha de prevenirse el mal*[14] or Guevara's *El espejo del mundo*, which are contemporary if not, in the case of *Cómo ha de usarse del bien*, older than Salucio del Poyo's dramas on Luna and Ruy Dávalos, set some important patterns for subsequent dramas on favorites.[15] In those two plays, the role played by fortune acting as an arbitrary supernatural force seems insignificant compared to the consequences derived from the characters' decisions and actions. The protagonists of *Cómo ha de usarse del bien* and *El espejo del mundo*, Payo de Guzmán and Don Basco de Portugal, are favored because they possess the virtues to be an appropriate royal favorite.[16] It is due to these virtues that they overcome certain vicissitudes, which are only associated with fortune's fluctuations by means of metaphors, and end being rewarded by the monarchs. In other words, both *Cómo ha de usarse del bien* and *El espejo del mundo* focus on the ideal qualities of a favorite minister and his ability to succeed rather than on an inevitable destiny dictated by fortune.

This emphasis on the virtues of the favorite coincides with Lerma's propagandistic agenda, which was intense during the first years of the seventeenth century, to legitimate his position as the king's favorite. As an example, one may read the octave verses written in honor of Lerma after he had become the patron of the University of Alcalá in 1606 (*Recibimiento*). Some of those poems insist on Lerma's prudence and on his ability to "domesticate" and stop the cycling of Fortune's wheel. Unlike the foolish or "necio," who rises and falls under fortune's control, Lerma is wise and possesses the virtue, which is compared to a sword, that "can chop off Fortune's head."[17] Due to this virtue, the poem concludes, Lerma deserves the favors that he receives from the king ("you [Lerma] deserved to be given the royal sword").[18]

This image of a wise royal favorite whose prudence, which is one of the values most venerated by Neostoics, justifies his position can be seen in *Cómo ha de usarse del bien* and *El espejo del mundo* as well as in other contemporary and later dramas on favorites – e.g. Lope's *La fortuna merecida* or Vélez de Guevara's *El Lucero de Castilla y Luna de Aragón* – intended to praise the figure of Lerma or, at least, to legitimate the existence of the royal favorite. Indeed, this type of propagandistic drama remains in vogue during the reign of Philip IV in plays like *Cómo ha de ser el privado*, in which Quevedo completely ignores the dramatic dichotomies and the two-side structure of fortune and focuses on presenting an ideal Neostoic favorite character who is "a transparent anagram of Olivares."[19] Therefore, early plays like *Cómo ha de usarse del bien* and *El espejo del mundo* are to a certain extent prototypes of a significant series of dramas underlining the ideal characteristics of royal favorites. Thus those plays are not prototypical because of their depiction of an unpredictable and determinant fortune but because of their focus on virtuous favorites who succeed to overcome fortune's fluctuations. One of the plays that more clearly shows this type of Neostoic favorite is the unstudied *La paciencia en la fortuna.*

La paciencia en la fortuna

La paciencia en la fortuna – henceforth referred to as *La paciencia* – is an early seventeenth-century play on royal favoritism that has so far received scarce attention from scholars. As I recently argued, this play was written around 1612 by Lope de Vega, the most prolific Spanish playwright of dramas on favorites, with the purpose of eulogizing the Duke of Lerma and his family (Gómez, "La paciencia"). At that moment in Spain dramas on favorites were in vogue, and Lope de Vega participated actively in this trend by means of his dramatic poetry, which for the most part contributed to vindicate the position of Philip III's royal favorite. As proof of Lope's leading role in this matter, one may consider the collection of plays that, although written by different authors, was published in 1612 under his name. The *Tercera parte de las comedias de Lope de Vega* included seven dramas on favorites, which suggests that it was organized according to a thematic criterion, unusual not only among the different *partes* of Lope's *comedias* but also in the history of Spanish printed dramas (Giuliani). George Peale regards this collection, which was reprinted twice (1613 and 1614), as a milestone in the history of political favoritism in Spanish drama and underlines the popularity of this topic during those years ("Comienzos").

Furthermore, during that same period, Lope had a major role as publicist of Lerma's politics and benefited from the lavish expenditure of wealth on court spectacles that the Duke put into effect (Wright; Pedraza). Some of Lope's plays were commissioned by Lerma himself and performed in the private spaces of the favorite's properties, which, in turn, were often described by Lope with words of admiration. *La paciencia*, which seems to have been originally conceived to celebrate the matrimonial union of Lerma's relatives before a courtly audience, would superbly fulfill the goals that Lope sought throughout those years. This play shows scenes of a wedding celebrated in the magnificent residence – called sometimes *huerta* (7, 8v, and 11),[20] as some of Lerma's properties were known – of a royal favorite, whose figure is also idealized. Moreover, it lauds the Moncada lineage as well as that of the Cerda, which are placed at the core of the Duke of Lerma's family and courtly politics.

In order to proceed further with the analysis of *La paciencia*, which remains unprinted, it seems appropriate to examine briefly the storyline of the play. As is usual in Spanish dramas on favorites, *La paciencia* is set in the Middle Ages, more precisely in fourteenth-century Aragon. The play begins with Manrique, a noble fugitive, trying to steal bread from a dog in the ducal palace of Gastón de Moncada, the protagonist of the play. Pantoja, the buffoon character and servant of the Duke, wants to punish the intruder but Gastón shows instead clemency and hospitality to him. Then King Pedro arrives to the estate of Gastón, who had been the royal favorite of King Pedro's father ("[Gastón] was the soul / of my father").[21] The king is impressed not only by Gastón's property, a dazzling palace surrounded by beautiful gardens, fountains, sculptures, and paintings, but also by his wife, the Duchess Violante de la Cerda. He immediately falls in love with Violante and tries in different ways to be alone with her without success. Gastón is offered to be the king's Master of the Horse, but the Duke declines in favor of Manrique who accepts this paramount office and promises to die for the hospitable and generous Gastón. This refusal of the Duke, interpreted by the king as arrogance, and the rejection of the Duchess to his amorous intentions exhaust the ire of the monarch who returns to the royal court with plans for revenge.

Following these plans, King Pedro showers Manrique with all of the titles, offices, and lands that belonged to Gastón and, at the same time, commands him to imprison the Duke, his wife, and their son Gastonino. These *contretemps* challenge Gastón's patience through to the end of the play. The situation of the Duke and the Duchess worsens to a pathetic degree when Manrique serves the couple a heart and a jug containing, they are told, their son's blood. Still in shock due to this devastating incident, Gastón also learns that the king has decreed his exile or death. In the end, and thanks to the cunning plan of Manrique who disguised the Queen María, spouse of King Pedro, as Violante, Gastón recovers his estates, titles, and family, including his son Gastonino, whose heart had been falsely replaced by that of a lamb.

Neostoicism

La paciencia exalts the character Gastón de Moncada, the ideal royal favorite. At the end of the play, when the king restores the political order and makes justice, Gastón is rewarded by the monarch for his patience:

> "I admire
> the patience you had
> on your fortune and, as a reward,
> I shall let you live."[22]

Patience is certainly Gastón's main feature and his weapon against fortune's fluctuations which are inherently linked with power. This conception of patience seems to have a strong flavor of stoic philosophy, and indeed this play may be related to the wide dissemination of Neostoicism that took place in Europe when the play was written.[23] Gastón's stoic nature is perfectly illustrated by the scene in which he is unjustly imprisoned in a tower, and, for dinner, they bring him a plate with a heart on it; moreover, instead of water they bring him blood. He is told that these are the heart and the blood of his son. Gastón goes through all of this and yet he does not rebel or lose control over himself; rather he makes a conscious effort to be patient: "Having passion is not prudent, / and since everything else is lost, / let us not lose patience."[24] He maintains his composure even when his wife Violante reproaches him with passivity by using gender stereotypes: "When I am the man, / you act like the woman."[25] Violante encourages her husband to kill Manrique, for in doing so he would avenge his son's murder and restore his honor. However, Gastón only reacts to his misfortunes with resignation and acceptance of the desired death, just like Socrates did at his trial, later becoming a role model for the Stoics.

Suffering adversity and forbearance are fundamental principles of Stoicism that define the essence of the protagonist of *La paciencia*. He is also a man who lives in accordance with virtue and nature in his country estate, surrounded by beautiful gardens, statues, and fountains and far from the tumultuous royal court. These features are modeled in accordance with the principles of the Neostoic philosophy. In one of Justus Lipsius' most celebrated books, *De Constantia* (1584), which was reprinted multiple times as well as translated into numerous languages, patience (*patientia*) is the mother of constancy (*constantia*).[26] Constancy is, according to Lipsius, the virtue to which all wise men should aspire, for constancy makes men free – they are only subjected to God – and inhibits them from the oppression of fortune, which Lipsius depicts as the enemy of Stoics. Therefore, wise men use their constancy – and patience, where constancy originates – to overcome the fluctuations of fortune. Furthermore, Lipsius adds, the most appropriate places to attain wisdom (*sapientia*) are gardens, where philosophers like to be in harmony with nature, surrounded by flowers, water, and beautiful marble. This idyllic mode of life was known in the Renaissance as *beatus ille*, an expression coming from the Latin poet Horace, whose work, along with that of Seneca and Tacitus, contributed largely to shape the principles of Neostoicism. Nevertheless, the idea of withdrawing from civil affairs to cultivate one's own garden is more Epicurean than Stoic, but Lipsius, who was ambiguous about the participation in public life, endorsed this idea in *De Constantia* (Corbett 150–1; Salmon 203).[27]

The relation of the Stoic philosopher to a natural space must be underscored because it might help to understand better those dramas featuring favorites who frequent or live in a natural environment. The protagonist of *La paciencia*, due to his intellectual abilities – especially his worship of patience–, may be regarded as an ideal stoic favorite. The author of this play, moreover, depicts Gastón de Moncada's estate as an idyllic place and emphasizes the attachment of Gastón to nature or *beatus ille*, insomuch as it is due to this attachment that Gastón refuses King Pedro's favors and does not offer to assist him in the royal court. The play provides details of the environment in which Gastón lives: its fountains, paintings, marbles, and even description of flowers, their colors, and how they are conceived in relation to painting (22v–23), all of these details remind of Lipsius' admiration for gardens in *De Constantia* (2.2).

These features that enable one to consider Gastón to be a model of Stoicism could just as easily cause one to consider him to be a philosopher favorite. This characterization would not be unique, given that it can be found in other dramas on royal favorites, for example in *Cómo ha de usarse del bien y ha de prevenirse el mal.*[28] This play shows a plot structure that is common to other dramas on favorites: at the beginning of a reign, the newly crowned king has problems with an incumbent royal favorite or with the latter's son – the new favorite. In *La paciencia* the new king, Pedro, confronts Gastón, the royal favorite of Pedro's father; in *Cómo ha de usarse del bien*, the newly crowned monarch Alfonso comes into conflict with Payo de Guzmán, whose father had served as favorite minister to the former king, Alfonso's father.

In the first act of *Cómo ha de usarse del bien*, which tells a story similar to that of *La paciencia*, the king and his courtiers visit Payo de Guzmán's estate, thus disrupting the serene atmosphere that the favorite minister enjoys. Payo de Guzmán, like Gastón, feels aversion for court affairs and is uncomfortable around courtiers, although in his case this feeling is even more intense than in Gastón. Payo, an Asturian nobleman, shows no interest in abandoning his peaceful and fulfilling rural life at Toral to serve the king at the turbulent and superficial court. He is not even willing to change his rustic clothes when fulfilling his duties at the royal palace. This bond with the countryside perfectly matches the stoic view of politics and life, so much so that Payo, likened to Diogenes (1.247) – a Greek thinker honored by the Stoics – is considered to be a philosopher (2.1006–7):

> "He banishes himself from court
> and lives like a philosopher
> at home, on his plot of land
> where all splendor is forbidden,
> expecting nothing from the sea
> created by human ambition."[29]

Here Payo is depicted as a wise man representing ideals of Neostoicism; by cultivating the virtue of austerity, he distrusts and overcomes capricious fortune. The sea is interpreted as a metaphor of fortune or court, where fortune's vicissitudes take place. The Italian word *fortuna*, in a literary sense, meant "storm," especially on the sea; this is how Dante, for example, used it often.[30] This interpretation of the word "fortune" became commonplace among many early modern writers (Rico 114) such as Lope de Vega (e.g. *Peregrino* 70) and employed another literary trope of a stoic nature, namely the navigator's motif. The navigator's motif, as conveyed by Horace or Seneca, compared the dangers of the sea to the challenges and threats that human beings face in life, and emphasized the constancy and self-restraint, the control of the passions, to overcome those difficulties.[31] Therefore the "sea" – this is fortune and, by extension, court – was seen as a dangerous place, amoral, and corrupt, against which a virtuous man defended. This is what Payo and Gastón, armed with stoic values such as self-control and patience, do to protect themselves from what they saw as the destructive vices of courtly life. Other Spanish dramas featuring favorites portray a similar situation. For example, in Vélez de Guevara's *El Lucero de Castilla y Luna de Aragón* (1613), the favorite the Duke of Arjona and his wife Aldonza anchor their senses to prudence in order to be safe in the agitated sea of the court:

> "Let us lash our senses
> to the helm of prudence,
> as the headwinds gust
> and this is an unfortunate squall
> of such rough tides!
> We shall triumph with prudence,
> which is the plank where life
> and honor attempt to survive!"[32]

The fact that fortune and court were represented as a stormy sea explains why the appointment of royal favorite was sometimes, as in the earlier text, compared to the oscillations of a boat on the water. The favorite minister, in order to succeed in his position, had to know how to navigate insecure waters, that is to say, competition, instability, hypocrisy, envy, flattery, and deception, just to name a few of the stereotypes that contemporary literature created about the vulnerabilities of courtly life. In this sense, stoic wisdom was, to many intellectuals, a persuasive guide for courtiers and, more specifically, for favorite ministers; stoic virtues functioned, one could say, as courtly virtues. However, stoic precepts, although significant, were only part of a larger body of knowledge intended to instruct courtiers and particularly the most ambitious of them, the favorites, on how to behave at court. From this perspective, the dramas on favorites, especially those dramas whose main characters followed stoic principles, can be read in the light of courtesy literature and the increasing trend of manuals of courtly conduct that, following the model of *Il libro del cortegiano* by Castiglione, developed throughout Europe during the sixteenth and seventeenth centuries (Whigham; Sieber, "Literary Continuity"; Álvarez-Ossorio; Goldsmith).

This aulic or courtly science experienced a prolific epoch between the end of the sixteenth century and the first decades of the seventeenth century in Spain. In this epoch, coinciding with the Duke of Lerma's rise to power and the transformation of the Spanish court, numerous advisory books centered on the courtiers' conduct were published. Given the context in which they were published, some of these works were specifically conceived of as manuals for ambitious ministers aspiring to consolidate or improve their positions. On occasion, they were dedicated to Lerma or one of his followers. The circumstances and purposes surrounding this courtesy literature are thus fairly similar to those of the dramas on favorites, and therefore many parallels can be drawn between the prose texts on the conduct of influential courtiers and the dramatic poetry depicting all-powerful ministers. In the following analysis, some non-dramatic texts will be discussed vis-à-vis *La paciencia* in order to delve into details of this play and the impact of Neostoicism in theater.

One of the most popular examples of courtly manuals was *La filosofía cortesana moralizada* (1587) by Alonso de Barros. Given that it was printed at least three times in the span of barely a year in two different courts, Madrid and Naples, and also may have reached the Spanish colonies of America, scholars suppose that Barros' work enjoyed widespread popularity (Infantes; Lucero). *La filosofía cortesana* was a book guiding and commenting on the courtier's career, but it was also accompanied by a board game tracing each of the steps of that career. The format of the game was similar to that of the *juego de la oca* (game of the goose), in which players threw dice and moved their game pieces forward through the numbered squares of the board; the goal of the game was to land on the last square and win the pot. The path in the board game devised by Barros, which was found recently in the British Library, symbolized the obstacles that a courtier encountered in his journey to success, and the "victory," as the final square was named, indicated the achievement of his aspirations.

In the preliminaries of *La filosofía cortesana*, the potential readers and contents of the book are metaphorically described in a sonnet written by Miguel de Cervantes: "He who navigates through the insane gulf / of the sea of aspirations."[33] This image of the court as "insane" waters and the courtier as a navigator is of great importance for Barros as well, for the center of the board game is decorated with the painting of a sea named, based on the moral principles inspiring Barros' writing, the Sea of Suffering ("Mar del Sufrimiento"). Barros explains, with words similar to those of Cervantes, that the name of the sea reflects the difficulties that those who have aspirations at court must face ("he who would engulf himself in this abyss of aspirations") and also highlights the decisiveness of patience to achieve those goals (50–1). From this perspective, the protagonist of *La paciencia*, Gastón, is shown to be an exemplary courtier both enduring the suffering and mastering the most important key to success in court, patience:

> "I challenge you, punishments,
> to come to me relentlessly.
> You would only prove
> my patience on fortune"[34]

Being patient, nevertheless, was not only valuable for fulfilling the needs of ambitious courtiers. As any other classical and pagan stoic value, patience was, in the early modern trend of Neostoicism, manipulated to conform to the principles of Christianity, and as a result, being patient became a Christian virtue. This is the lesson that one could learn in *Proverbios morales* (1598), another didactic book by Alonso de Barros concerning ethics: "There is no better way to please / God than being patient" (990, p. 56).

Proverbios morales, like *La filosofía cortesana*, was reprinted repeatedly and translated into French within the decades after its first publication. Barros, who was appointed to various royal offices throughout his life (1542–1604), was a well-established man in court and enjoyed the friendship of distinguished intellectuals and writers. *La filosofía cortesana* was introduced to its readers by Miguel de Cervantes, and the preliminaries of *Proverbios morales* included a poem composed in *redondillas* by Lope de Vega ("Este libro es un Diamante"), who obviously was familiar with Barros' work and could have used it to shape the character of Gastón in *La paciencia*.

Another friend of Barros was Hernando de Soto, with whom he shared his fondness for emblems and moral philosophy. Soto participated in the eulogies of *Proverbios morales* as well and, in turn, Barros wrote a eulogy for Soto's *Emblemas moralizadas* (1599). Hernando de Soto was also a courtly man and made a successful career under the shadow of the Duke of Lerma, to whom he dedicated his *Emblemas*. The last emblem of this book, as a matter of fact, was an explicit celebration of Lerma's *valimiento* or position as the royal favorite (127–8). Some scholars suggest that Lerma acted as Soto's patron in the Spanish court, and his *Emblemas*, along with Sebastián de Covarrubias' *Emblemas morales* (1610), have been studied as part of the large group of works intended to defend Lerma's position (Tropé, "Valimiento y mecenazgo"). In that group, of course, there were many dramatic texts, and *La paciencia* seems to be one of them.

Praising the favorite, in this epoch, was something ordinary and a common denominator for a group of writers sharing interests and connected in multiple ways. Hernando de Soto was a close friend of Lope de Vega; he wrote preliminary poems for Lope's *Arcadia* (1598) and *Isidro* (1599); and Lope used Soto's *Emblemas moralizadas* as a source to compose verses of his *La Dragontea* (1598) (1.42.331–2). Their friendship and the use of Soto's *Emblemas* by Lope, together with the fact that this book was addressed to the Duke of Lerma, lend evidence that Lope was the author of *La paciencia*, since the dramatist could have molded the main character of this play based on an emblem from Soto's work.

Indeed, one of the first emblems of Hernando de Soto discusses the concept of patience.[35] Here the author emphasizes the benefits of being patient and the importance of suffering. In this regard, he offers the examples of the ancient Greek Socrates and the biblical figure Job, thus linking the classical and Christian traditions which characterize the Neostoic movement. This mixture of Stoic ethics and Christian principles seems to be concentrated in the figure of Gastón de Moncada.

Soto's arguments on the theme of patience were expanded in a later and less known book, *Desengaño de fortuna* (1611) by Gutierre Marqués de Careaga. Judging by the date provided by Careaga at the end of the text, in 1606 this book had already been written, but it was not published until 1611 in Barcelona and was reprinted in Madrid a year later, approximately when *La paciencia* must have been written. Careaga dedicated his work to Rodrigo Calderón, probably the most powerful minister of the Duke of Lerma and an inspiration for many dramas on favorites (MacCurdy).

In *Desengaño de fortuna*, Careaga's purpose was to reject the classical notion of Fortune as a divinity determining people's fate and to substitute it with the Christian notion of Providence. With this aim, he used and cited the works by Alonso de Barros and Hernando de Soto, so much so that the title of his book reminds of *Desengaño de cortesanos; Le désabus des courtisans*, a bilingual Spanish-French edition of Barros' *Proverbios morales* published in Paris in 1617. For the purpose of Careaga's book, patience, where the true disillusionment – *desengaño* – of fortune is (143), played an important role. Careaga expanded on what his predecessors had already stated about this topic, adding a special emphasis on the Christian perspective. This perspective offers, in turn, a new interpretation of *La paciencia*, since Gastón de Moncada may be seen, in addition to an ideal Stoic, as an exemplary Christian.

The title chosen by Careaga for his treatise is far from vague, for the word *desengaño* has a rich meaning in seventeenth-century Spanish culture. According to Jane Albrecht, who studies this concept in the light of the impact of Stoicism in Spanish tragedy, *desengaño* "means coming to consciousness and accepting a radical transformation, often imminent downfall or death, and also cognizance of the truth and necessity of conversion" (*Stoicism* 40). This conversion, in the case of Careaga's work, means the replacement of the pagan belief in the divinity of Fortune with the Christian notion of Providence. In *La paciencia*, the structure of the play shows also that conversion or, rather, the triumph of the Christian dogma over the ancient logic of Stoicism. Gastón de Moncada, throughout the play, shows a stoic attitude toward adversity, and following that attitude, the reasonable thing to do would be to accept and even wish for his death. This is, in fact, what Gastón wants in the first place:

> "If living and feeling
> are the causes of my anguish,
> my death feels like a relief,
> because if I die
> I'm excused from feeling.
> Let the murderer come"[36]

However, Manrique prevents Gastón from realizing his wish to die and claims that only God is entitled to give and take people's lives: "You do not know / you are being discourteous to God."[37] Later on, again Manrique, playing the role of a divine messenger, enlightens King Pedro who admits his mistakes and addresses him with these words: "God sends you / to open my eyes / to my own illusions."[38] Finally, and thanks to Manrique's mediation, the king rewards Gastón's patience by absolving him of a death sentence and allowing him to live. In this sense, the character of the king, which in Spanish drama and especially in Lope's works was often considered to be a sacred figure (Young 71–109; Crapotta 45), is seen as a representation of God on Earth. There is no contradiction between the human and faulty attitude of King Pedro throughout the play and his divine role, at the end, as guarantor of justice and restorer of order. In fact, in Lope's dramas the character of the monarch generally resolves himself the problems derived from the abuse of royal power, since the king, like Pedro in *La paciencia*, "realizes his errors and corrects his own behavior" (Crapotta 37).

The third act of *La paciencia* displays this transformation of the characters and the final triumph of Christianity in relation to the monarchy. In the first conversation of that act, which takes place between Gastón and his servant Pantoja, the former seems to predict changes to come: "These have been today, Pantoja, / the disillusionments of the world."[39] Here Gastón, following Albrecht's definition of *desengaño*, shows himself to be conscious of his poor situation and fall from grace, while announcing a radical change or conversion. This change comes at the very end of the play when the word *engaño* is repeated up to five times throughout the last scene. Gastón, in this regard, is a truly Neostoic character, one who follows Stoic principles accommodated to the Christian dogma. He remains alive, in spite of his thoughts about dying and the fact that Stoicism allowed for suicide, because Christianity, and Lipsius (Salmon 204), condemned this idea and taught that only God ends people's life.

In *Desengaño de fortuna*, the suffering of being patient is compared to a martyrdom that brings one closer to God, since it is God who puts people under strain: "Through death and martyrdom He pays for the good lives of his servants" (152v). This Christian notion of a divine trial for certain individuals is a heritage grounded in Stoicism, according to which "the gods single out the best among us for punishment" (Albrecht, *Stoicism* 58). In *La paciencia*, by underlining the patience of a favorite living in abundance and his ability to suffer throughout the play, the playwright shows the stoic virtues of Gastón and prepares the final idea that he is a saint.[40] To reach such a conclusion, the dramatist combines both Stoic and Christian elements in the same way that Careaga does in his Neostoic *Desengaño de fortuna*. In Chapter 17, Careaga examines the value of patience and uses as examples the lives of Socrates and Job. About the first, Careaga tells two anecdotes showing the stoicism of the Greek philosopher: the first anecdote stresses how Socrates remained impassive while his wife scolded and insulted him; in the second anecdote, Socrates continued giving a speech in a public square after learning that one of his sons had died (158). These two anecdotes find a dramatic parallel in *La paciencia* in the scene in which Gastón is told that his son is dead: holding a knife in one hand and, he thinks, his son's heart in the other hand, he controls his anger and refrains from attacking Manrique, the supposed architect of his disgraces, despite the fact that a defiant Violante encourages him to kill Manrique and curses him for not doing it (40–1). Immediately after the anecdotes about Socrates,

Careaga tells the biblical story of how Job's patience and constancy were tested when he lost his wealth, livestock, servants, friends, and children as well as his wife's respect for him. Job assumed that all he had was a gift from God and therefore God was entitled to retrieve it. What did offend Job was, however, to be accused by his friends of being a sinner. At the end Job, who was "one of God's greatest favorites," was rewarded by God because of his exemplary faith and patience (160). Likewise, King Pedro, acting tyrannically, deprives Gastón of his servants, titles, and properties, and yet Gastón finds no reason to blame the king, but he only laments being accused of treason:

> "He owns me, my estate,
> my wealth and my honor.
> Yet I am only saddened
> to be called a traitor."[41]

When Violante warns him of the beginning of persecutions, he replies:

> "No persecution
> will close my mouth.
> Under these circumstances,
> wise men show
> their patience on fortune."[42]

Indeed, from this moment until the end of the play, with great difficulty and suffering due to the king's decisions to kill his son and separating him from his wife, Gastón manages to remain patient and being finally rewarded for it. Until this moment, the king had acted evilly, without having control over his passions, just like in the biblical story it was the Devil, with God's approval, who caused Job's disgraces. Therefore Gastón, like Job, is martyrized until the king, rectifying and acting justly like God, rewards him for his patience.

That the author of *La paciencia* associates the favorite character to a saint should not be surprising. This depiction of a sacred favorite is even more meaningful in the context of a play intended to exalt the figure of the Duke of Lerma. In fact, Lope de Vega had already attempted to sacralize the position of the royal favorite in two *autos sacramentales*: *La privanza del hombre* and *Las bodas entre el Alma y el Amor divino*. In this last auto, as well as in *Romance a las venturosas bodas que se celebraron en la insigne ciudad de Valencia*, Lope compared the Duke of Lerma to St John the Baptist,[43] thus emphasizing the role of the saint-favorite as servant and advisor to Christ-king. This comparison can also be seen in contemporary sermons, poems, and political treatises, in addition to an increasing number of paintings and sculptures of John the Baptist during the years in which Lerma, who commissioned many of these artistic objects, was the favorite of Philip III.[44]

In conclusion, *La paciencia* is a propagandistic play depicting a royal favorite whose loyalty and virtues are prized by the monarch. In this regard, this play follows a pattern common in Spanish dramas on favorites that associate their protagonists to Neostoic virtues. More precisely, this Neostoic influence results in the depiction of Senecan favorites, for instance in Ruiz de Alarcón plays concerning favoritism (Campbell, "El poder"), since in seventeenth-century Spain the life and works of the Cordovan Seneca had a greater impact than any other classical author promoted by Lipsius and the Neostoics. In addition to his moral philosophy, the importance of Seneca was also due to his works as a dramatist, which were widely known through the Latin edition of his tragedies by Lipsius (Albrecht, *Stoicism* 70). The dramatic work of Lope de Vega, who translated passages of those tragedies, was highly influenced by Neostoicism and particularly by Seneca, as Albrecht has recently studied, and that influence may also be extended to *La paciencia*, which includes references to famous Senecan characters such as Medea and Phaedra (34v) as well as scenes that recall Senecan dramas. For instance, when Gastón is in prison and told that his son is dead (40), this reminds the reader of the bloody feast of the tragedy of Thiseas. However, unlike Thiseas, Gastón does not drink the blood of his son, who is otherwise alive, because *La paciencia* is not a tragedy and it finally shows a Christian message of salvation that is absent in the works of Seneca. In this sense, this Neostoic play is also an early treatment of the Christianization of Stoicism, a topic that is largely developed in later Spanish works, notably in Francisco de Quevedo's *Providencia de Dios* and *La constancia y paciencia del santo Job* (Ettinghausen; Blüher 427–86).

These Senecan attributes that are seen in the protagonist of *La paciencia* find parallels in the representation of royal favoritism in *Le Favori, ou la Coquette*, which will be discussed in the following chapter, although they contrast with the depiction of the title character of *Sejanus*, which is discussed in Chapter 4.

Notes

1 Cf. Feros, "El viejo monarca," who emphasizes a continuity between the situation of *juntas* and favorites during the 1580s and 1590s and what emerged after Philip II.
2 Feros, *El Duque de Lerma* 227. Cf. Alvar 343ff.
3 See Schroth 103–4 for more examples in which Lerma imitates the artistic representation of the Spanish monarchs.
4 *La privanza y caída de don Álvaro de Luna* (c. 1601), *La próspera fortuna de Ruy López Dávalos* (c. 1603), and *La adversa fortuna de Ruy López Dávalos* (c. 1603).
5 Knoll 71–2. In Spain, Boccaccio's *De Casibus* was translated as *Caída de príncipes*.
6 Lope cites it simply as *Próspera y adversa fortuna* (*El peregrino* 171).
7 Some examples are Salucio del Poyo's *La próspera* and *La adversa fortuna de Ruy López Dávalos* (c. 1603), Mira de Amescua's *La próspera* and *La adversa fortuna de don Bernardo de Cabrera* (c. 1620), Cordero's *La próspera* and *La*

adversa fortuna de Duarte Pacheco (c. 1621), and Amescua's *La próspera* and *La adversa fortuna de don Álvaro de Luna* (1621–24).

8 Some of those scholars are Cauvin, Bradner, Caparrós, *Entre validos y letrados* and "Privado," Oriel, Ferrer 162–3, and Mrozek 110–1.

9 See González's introduction to Vélez de Guevara's *El Lucero de Castilla*, 19.

10 Among these dramas are *Cómo ha de usarse del bien y ha de prevenirse el mal* (c. 1600), Lope's *La fortuna merecida* (1603), Tirso's *Privar contra su gusto* (c. 1621), Quevedo's *Cómo ha de ser el privado* (c. 1629), and Vélez de Guevara's *El espejo del mundo* (c. 1602), *El Lucero de Castilla y luna de Aragón* (1613), and *El conde don Pero Vélez y Sancho el Deseado* (1615).

11 For a detailed discussion on the tragic nature of dramas on favorites in Spain, see also Teulade.

12 According to Serrano, "such works lack a deep and individualized analysis of the royal favorite. Instead, they provide a generalization of the character followed by a severe warning on the transience of goods, glories, and earthly powers, always subject to the capricious and unstable Fortune" (535).

13 Teulade also diminishes the role of fortune in favor of the power struggles between monarchs and favorites (esp. 108). More recently, Peale has analyzed Ruiz de Alarcón's multiple dramas on favorites in which the theme of fortune is not a driving force and notes that Alarcón does not dramatize the rise and fall of favorites ("Los principios" 26).

14 This play, whose text has been preserved only in a manuscript copy in the Biblioteca Palatina di Parma, is also known as *Los Guzmanes de Toral* because it was first attributed to Lope de Vega, who listed that title in *El peregrino en su patria*. However, in Paola Laskaris' most recent edition it appears as anonymous. I wish to thank Professor Laskaris for sending me a copy of her edition.

15 Recently, Carl Wise has pointed out significant differences between Salucio del Poyo's and later dramas on favorites: "Salucio's overtly 'flawed' *privado* is unique, as both Lope and Mira seem to completely ignore any negative characteristics associated with historical *privados*" (23). Nevertheless, Wise's analysis is limited to five plays by Lope and Mira de Amescua of the early 1620s.

16 On Don Basco, Sieber says that he "is the perfect royal minister" and "The story of his rise to power could easily be a description of Duke of Lerma's ascent" ("The Magnificent Fountain" 103).

17 "cortar puede a fortuna la cabeza" (fol. 15).

18 "mereció que se os diese el real estoque" (fol. 15).

19 Elliott, *The Count-Duke of Olivares* 281, and 278–95 on Olivares as "the new Spanish Seneca." Luciana Gentilli defines Quevedo's play as a "journalistic play" (*comedia noticiera*) in the introduction to her edition (13), and Cauvin states that the sole purpose of this play is the eulogy of Olivares "in a drama almost entirely devoid of conflict or opposition in the dramatic sense" (374). On the dramatic deficiencies of the play, see also Profeti 126–9.

20 All citations from *La paciencia*, except where otherwise noted, refer to the manuscript preserved in the Biblioteca Palatina di Parma. The parenthetical numbering refers to folio. For details on the textual history of this play, see Gómez, "La paciencia."

21 "Alma fue / de mi padre don Gastón" (12).

22

"me admira
la paciencia que has tenido
en tu fortuna y querría
darte con que vivas." (52v)

23 On the influence of Neostoicism in Spanish literature, see Ettinghausen, who focuses on Quevedo's work, and Krabbenhoft, who includes the analysis of dramas concerning favorites such as Tirso de Molina's *El vergonzoso en palacio* and Ruiz de Alarcón's *Los pechos privilegiados*. More recently, Albrecht has studied Seneca's influence on Spanish tragedy (*Stoicism*) and Campbell has analyzed the Neostoicism in several plays by Calderón de la Barca (*La vida*) and Ruiz de Alarcón's dramas on favorites ("El dueño" and "El poder").

24 "Tener pasión no es prudencia, / y pues todo se ha perdido, / no se pierda la paciencia" (41v).

25 "que cuando yo soy el hombre, / tú pareces la mujer" (40v).

26 I use the Spanish translation –*Libro de la constancia*– by Juan Bautista de Mena, published in Seville in 1616.

27 No less important were, in this regard, the works praising the virtues of the countryside in contrast to the life at court, most notably Antonio de Guevara's *Menosprecio de corte y alabanza de aldea* (1539), a book that was reprinted multiple times in Spanish and translated into French, English, Italian, and German throughout the sixteenth and seventeenth centuries (Karl).

28 On the protagonist of *Cómo ha de usarse del bien* as a Stoic philosopher and wise man living in a rural ambience, see Hildner.

29

> "De la corte se destierra
> y cual filósofo vive
> en su casa, en su solar
> donde las pompas prohíbe
> sin esperar en el mar
> que humana ambición concibe." (1.258–62)

30 "come nave in fortuna" ("like a ship caught in a storm"), *Purgatorio* 32.116. Translated by J. Nichols (Alma Classics, 2017).

31 See Ana Isabel Sanchez's and Delphine Amstutz's commentaries on Lope de Vega, *La fortuna merecida* 136–49, and Dejardins, *Le Favori, ou la Coquette* 2.2.473–83, respectively.

32

> "¡Amarrémonos, sentidos,
> al timón de la prudencia,
> que corren vientos contrarios
> y esta es fortuna deshecha,
> y de mareta tan brava!
> ¡Triunfemos con la prudencia,
> que es tabla donde la vida
> y el honor salvarse intentan!" (1297–1304)

33 "El que navega por el golfo insano / del mar de pretensiones."

34

> "vengan en mí a dar
> penas sin cesar ninguna,
> que en ellas he de probar
> mi paciencia en la fortuna." (41v)

35 "Patience resolves and overcomes anything" ("Todo lo acaba y vence la paciencia") (15v-17).

36

> "Si está en vivir mi tormento
> y es mi tormento el sentir,

descanso en la muerte siento,
pues ahora con morir
me escusa del sentimiento.
Venga el dichoso homicida." (41v)

37 "No sabes / que eres a Dios descortés" (43).
38 "os envía / Dios para que abra los ojos / del engaño en que vivía" (52).
39 "Estos hoy, Pantoja, han sido / los desengaños del mundo" (36).
40 I refer to the interpretation that the editors of Lope's *El ejemplo de casadas y prueba de la paciencia* offer for this play focused on Laurencia's patience: "By emphasizing through such theatrical methods the 'martyrized' wife's patience and her ability to suffer, Lope prepares de final idea that this woman is a saint" ("Recalcar con tales modalidades teatrales la paciencia y la capacidad para sufrir de la esposa 'martirizada' es preparar la idea final de que esta mujer es una santa") (40). Similarities between *El ejemplo de casadas* and *La paciencia* are discussed in Gómez, "La paciencia" 76–9.
41

"Suyo soy, suyo es mi estado,
suya mi hacienda y mi honor.
Pero sólo me ha pesado
de que me llame traidor." (25v)

42

"Ninguna
desenfrenará mis labios,
así en muchas como en una,
que muestran los hombres sabios,
la paciencia en la fortuna." (26)

43 See lines 93–7 of the *Romance*, which is appended to Lope's *Fiestas de Denia*, and the commentaries by Bernardo García (212). On Lope's encomiastic depiction of Lerma as John the Baptist in *Las bodas entre el Alma y el Amor divino*, which is placed at the end of the second book of *El peregrino en su patria*, see Feros, *El Duque de Lerma* 193–4.
44 Banner 30 and 86. Quevedo, among others political commentators, wrote on the figure of St. John the Baptist as a model of favorite minister (*Política de Dios* 69–75).

Works Cited

Albrecht, Jane. *Stoicism, Seneca and Seventeenth-Century Spanish Tragedy*. Scripta Humanistica, 2012.
Alvar, Alfredo. *El Duque de Lerma: Corrupción y desmoralización en la España del siglo XVII*. Esfera de los Libros, 2010.
Álvarez-Ossorio, Antonio. "El cortesano discreto: Itinerario de una ciencia áulica (ss. XVI-XVII)." *Historia Social*, vol. 28, 1997, pp. 73–94.
Banner, Lisa. *The Religious Patronage of the Duke of Lerma, 1598–1621*. Ashgate, 2009.
Barros, Alonso de. *Filosofía cortesana moralizada*. Joseph Cacchij, 1588.
———. *Proverbios morales*. 1598. 3rd ed. Alonso Martín, 1608.
Blüher, Karl. *Séneca en España: Investigaciones sobre la recepción de Séneca en España desde el siglo XIII hasta el siglo XVII*. 1969. Edited by Juan Conde, Gredos, 1983.

Bradner, Leicester. "The Theme of *privanza* in Spanish and English Drama 1590–1625." *Homenaje a William L. Fichter. Estudios sobre teatro antiguo hispánico y otros ensayos*, edited by A. David Kossoff and José Amor, Castalia, 1971, pp. 97–106.

Cabrera de Córdoba, Luis. *Relaciones de las cosas sucedidas en la corte de España desde 1599 hasta 1614*. J. Martín Alegría, 1857.

Campbell, Ysla. "*El dueño de las estrellas* y *La amistad castigada*: dos dramas de privanza extremos." *Alarconiana: Estudios sobre la obra de Juan Ruiz de Alarcón*, edited by Y. Campbell, Universidad Autónoma de Ciudad Juárez, 2015, pp. 55–64.

———. "El poder y la privanza: las propuestas de Alarcón." *eHumanista*, vol. 32, 2016, pp. 201–19.

———. La vida es sueño *a la luz del pensamiento neoestoico-tacitista*. El Colegio de México, 2009.

Caparrós, Luis. *Entre validos y letrados: La obra dramática de Damián Salucio del Poyo*. Universidad de Valladolid, 1987.

———. "Privado." *Diccionario de la comedia del Siglo de Oro*, edited by Frank Casa et al., Castalia, 2001, pp. 240–2.

Careaga, Gutierre de. *Desengaño de fortuna*. Francisco Dotil, 1611.

Cauvin, Mary Austin. *The* comedia de privanza *in the Seventeenth Century*. Dissertation, U of Pennsylvania, 1957.

Centenera, Fernando. "Últimas confidencias entre Mariana y García de Loaysa: la grandeza de un arzobispado tan efímero como sus esperanzas para con el poder real." *Ingenium*, vol. 10, 2016, pp. 59–74.

Cómo ha de usarse del bien y ha de prevenirse el mal. Edited by Paola Laskaris, Mauro Baroni, 2008.

Corbett, Theodore. "The Cult of Lipsius: A Leading Source of Early Modern Spanish Statecraft." *Journal of the History of Ideas*, vol. 36, no. 1, 1975, pp. 139–52.

Crapotta, James. *Kingship and Tyranny in the Theater of Guillen de Castro*. Tamesis, 1984.

Elliott, John. *The Count-Duke of Olivares: The Statesman in an Age of Decline*. Yale UP, 1986.

Ettinghausen, Henry. *Francisco de Quevedo and the Neostoic Movement*. Oxford UP, 1972.

Feros, Antonio. *El Duque de Lerma: Realeza y privanza en la España de Felipe III*. Marcial Pons, 2002.

———. "El viejo monarca y los nuevos favoritos: los discursos sobre la privanza en el reinado de Felipe II." *Studia Historica. Historia Moderna*, vol. 17, 1997, pp. 11–36.

Ferrer Valls, Teresa. "El juego del poder: Lope de Vega y los dramas de la privanza." *Modelos de vida en la España del Siglo de Oro*, vol. 1, edited by I. Arellano and M. Vitse, Iberoamericana, 2004, pp. 159–85.

Giuliani, Luigi. "La tercera parte: historia editorial." *Comedias de Lope de Vega. Parte III*. Vol. 1, Milenio, 2002, pp. 11–48.

Goldsmith, Elizabeth C. *"Exclusive Conversations:" The Art of Interaction in Seventeenth-Century France*. U of Pennsylvania P, 1988.

Gómez Martos, Francisco. *La creación de una historia nacional. Juan de Mariana y el papel de la Antigüedad en la Edad Moderna*. Instituto de Historiografía Julio Caro Baroja, 2018.

———. "*La paciencia en la fortuna*: An Unprinted Play by Lope de Vega." *Arte nuevo. Revista de estudios áureos*, vol. 6, 2019, pp. 57–89.

Guevara, Antonio de. *Menosprecio de Corte y Alabanza de Aldea; Arte de Marear*. Edited by Asunción Rallo, Cátedra, 1984.

Gutiérrez, Jesús. *La* fortuna bifrons *en el teatro del Siglo de Oro*. Sociedad Menéndez Pelayo, 1975.

Hildner, David. "*Los Guzmanes de Toral*: valimiento y rusticidad en un drama lopesco." *Laberinto*, vol. 8, 2015, pp. 4–14.

Infantes, Víctor. "'Una pintura que se contiene en un pliego grande.' El tablero de la *Filosofía cortesana* de Alonso de Barros: una *Oca* emblemática entre España e Italia (1587 y 1588)." *Imago*, no. 2, 2010, pp. 127–135.

Karl, Louis. "Note sur la fortune des œuvres d'Antonio de Guevara à l'étranger." *Bulletin Hispanique*, vol. 35, no. 1, 1933, pp. 32–50.

Knoll, Robert. *Ben Jonson's Plays: An Introduction*. U of Nebraska P, 1964.

Krabbenhoft, Kenneth. *Neoestoicismo y género popular*. Universidad de Salamanca, 2001.

La paciencia en la fortuna. CC*IV 28033, *Comedias de Diferentes Autores*, vol. 74, no. 2. Biblioteca Palatina di Parma, Parma. 1–55r.

La privanza desleal y voluntad por la fama. T-55293-21 (provisional catalog number). Biblioteca Nacional de España, Madrid. 46–67v.

Lipsius, Justus. *Libro de la constancia*. Translated by Juan Bautista, Matías Clavijo, 1616.

Lucero, Ernesto. "Las ediciones antiguas de la *Filosofía cortesana* de Alonso de Barros. Una historia del texto." *Criticón*, vol. 127, 2016, pp. 169–95.

MacCurdy, Raymond. *The Tragic Fall: Don Álvaro de Luna and Other Favorites in Spanish Golden Age Drama*. U of North Carolina P, 1978.

Mariana, Juan de. *De rege et regis institutione libri III*, Pedro Rodríguez, 1599.

———. *Historiae de rebus Hispaniae*, Pedro Rodríguez, 1592.

———. *Tractatus septem*, A. Hierato, 1609.

Mira de Amescua, Antonio. *La adversa fortuna de don Álvaro de Luna*. Edited by M. González and M. C. García. *Teatro completo*. Vol. 6, edited by A. de la Granja, Universidad de Granada, 2001, pp. 117–225.

———. *La próspera* and *La adversa fortuna de don Bernardo de Cabrera*. Edited by A. Serrano. *Teatro completo*. Vol. 3, edited by A. de la Granja, Universidad de Granada, 2003, pp. 23–326.

Mrozek, Giuseppe. Validos *sotto accusa. Azioni giuridiche e dibattito culturale sul* valimiento *nel regno di Filippo III*. Dissertation, Università degli studi Roma Tre, 2012.

Oriel, Charles. "The Play of Presence and Absence: Writing and Supplementarity in the *Comedias de Privanza*." *"El arte nuevo de estudiar comedias:" Literary Theory and Spanish Golden Age Drama*, edited by Barbara Simerka, Bucknell UP, 1996, pp. 36–51.

Peale, C. George. "Comienzos, enfoques y constitución de la comedia de privanza en la *Tercera parte de las comedias de Lope de Vega y otros auctores*." *Hispanic Review*, vol. 72, no. 1, 2004, pp. 125–56.

———. "Los principios de la comedia de privanza y la vuelta genérica de Ruiz de Alarcón. Nuevos bocetos y nuevas directrices." *Alarconiana IV: Estudios sobre la obra de Juan Ruiz de Alarcón*, edited by Ysla Campbell and Édgar García, Universidad Autónoma de Ciudad Juárez, 2017, pp. 11–36.

Pedraza, Felipe. "Lope, Lerma y su duque a través del epistolario y varias comedias." *Dramaturgia festiva y cultura nobiliaria en el siglo de oro*, edited by B. García and M. L. Lobato, Iberoamericana, 2007, pp. 269–89.

Pellicer, Casiano. *Tratado histórico sobre el origen y progreso de la comedia y del histrionismo en España: Con las censuras teológicas, reales resoluciones y providencias del Consejo Supremo sobre comedias*. 1804. Edited by José María Díez Borque, Editorial Labor, 1975.

Profeti, María G. "Funciones teatrales y literarias del personaje del privado." Tropé, pp. 113–29.

Quevedo, Francisco de. *Cómo ha de ser el privado*. Edited by L. Gentilli, Mauro Baroni, 2004.

———. *Política de Dios y gobierno de Cristo*. 2nd ed. Espasa-Calpe, 1947.

Recibimiento al Excmo. Sr. D. Francisco de Rojas y Sandoval, Duque de Lerma ... por el Colegio Mayor y Universidad de Alcalá el día que vino a tomar posesión de patrón del dicho Colegio y Universidad. 1606. MS 6204. Biblioteca Nacional de España, Madrid. 3–28.

Rico, Francisco. "Para el prólogo del *Lazarillo*: 'El deseo de Alabanza'". *Picaresque Espagnole: Actes*. Centre d'études sociocritiques, 1976, pp. 101–16.

Salmon, J. H. M. "Stoicism and Roman Example: Seneca and Tacitus in Jacobean England." *Journal of the History of Ideas*, vol. 50, no. 2, 1989, pp. 199–225.

Salucio del Poyo, Damián. *La adversa fortuna de don Ruy López de Ávalos*. *Dramáticos contemporáneos de Lope de Vega*, vol. 43.1, edited by R. de Mesonero Romanos, M. Rivadeneyra, 1857, pp. 465–89.

———. *La privanza y caída de don Álvaro de Luna*. *Comedias*, edited by Carmen Hernández, Academia Alfonso X el Sabio, 1985, pp. 239–376.

———. *La próspera fortuna de don Ruy López de Ávalos*. *Dramáticos contemporáneos de Lope de Vega*, vol. 43.1, edited by R. de Mesonero Romanos, M. Rivadeneyra, 1857, pp. 437–63.

Schroth, Sarah. *The private picture collection of the Duke of Lerma*. Dissertation, New York U, 1990.

Serrano, Antonio. "Dos notas sobre comedias de validos en Mira de Amescua." *Mira de Amescua en canderelo*. Vol. 1, edited by A. de la Granja and J. A. Martínez, Universidad de Granada, 1996, pp. 533–43.

Sieber, Harry. "Literary Continuity, Social Order, and the Invention of the Picaresque." *Cultural Authority in Golden Age Spain*, edited by Marina Brownlee and Hans Ulrich Gumbrecht, Johns Hopkins UP, 1995, pp. 143–64.

———. "The Magnificent Fountain: Literary Patronage at the Court of Philip III." *Cervantes*, vol. 18, no. 2, 1998, pp. 85–116.

Soto, Hernando de. *Emblemas Moralizadas*. Edited by Carmen Bravo-Villasante, Fundación Universitaria Española, 1983.

Suárez, José Luis. *Teatro y toros en el Siglo de Oro español: Estudios sobre la licitud de la fiesta*. Universidad de Granada, 2003.

Teulade, Anne. "Le théâtre du doble: la réception de la *Comedia de privanza* entre tragédie et tragi-comédie." *Le théâtre espagnol du Siècle d'Or en France (XVIIe-XXe siècle). De la traduction au transfert culturel*, edited by Christophe Couderc, Presses Universitaires de Paris Ouest, 2012, pp. 101–15.

Tropé, Hélène, editor. *La représentation du favori dans l'Espagne de Philippe III et de Philippe IV*, Presses Sorbonne nouvelle, 2010.

———. "Valimiento y mecenazgo. Los artistas y los escritores ante el Duque de Lerma, valido de Felipe III (1598–1621)." Tropé, pp. 131–80.

Vaccari, Debora. *La dilogia su Cola di Rienzo del* licenciado *Juan Grajal*. Alinea, 2011.

Vega, Lope de. *Arcadia, prosas y versos*. Edited by Antonio Sánchez, Cátedra, 2012.

———. *El ejemplo de casadas y prueba de la paciencia. Comedias de Lope de Vega. Parte V*. Edited by Marie-Françoise Déodat-Kessedjian and Emmanuelle Garnier, Milenio, 2004, pp. 35–157.

———. *El peregrino en su patria*. Edited by Juan Bautista Avalle-Arce, Castalia, 1973.

———. *Fiestas de Denia*. Edited by M. G. Profeti and B. García García, Alinea, 2004.

———. *Isidro*. Edited by Antonio Sánchez, Cátedra, 2010.

———. *La Dragontea*. Edited by Antonio Sánchez, Cátedra, 2007.

———. *La fortuna merecida. Comedias. Parte XI*. Vol. 2. Edited by Ana Isabel Sánchez, Gredos, 2012, pp. 611–783.

———. *La privanza del hombre*. MS 17017. Biblioteca Nacional de España, Madrid. 3–28.

Vélez de Guevara, Luis. *El conde don Pero Vélez y don Sancho el Desaedo*. Edited by W. Manson and G. Peale, introduction by T. Case, Juan de la Cuesta, 2002.

———. *El espejo del mundo*. Edited by W. Manson and G. Peale, introduction by M. G. Profeti, Juan de la Cuesta, 2002.

———. *El Lucero de Castilla y Luna de Aragón*. Edited by W. Manson and G. Peale, introductions by J. J. González and G. Davies, Juan de la Cuesta, 2013.

Whigham, Frank. *Ambition and Privilege: the Social Tropes of Elizabethan Courtesy Theory*, U of California P, 1984.

Wise, Carl. *Shadow of the King: Privanza and Perceptions of Royal Power in Seventeenth-Century Spanish Theater*. Dissertation, U of Georgia, 2011.

Wright, Elizabeth. *Pilgrimage to Patronage: Lope de Vega and the Court of Philip III, 1598–1621*. Bucknell UP, 2001.

Young, Richard. *La Figura del Rey y la Institución Real en la Comedia Lopesca*. Ediciones José Porrúa Turanzas, 1979.

3 Favorites in French drama

In late sixteenth-century France, King Henri III (1574–89) surrounded himself with a group of favorite ministers known as *mignons*. This circumstance gave occasion to a varied discourse on the topic of favoritism, including two of the earliest plays dealing with this topic: Pierre Matthieu's *La Guisiade* (1589) and Simon Belyard's *Le Guysien* (1592), which commented on the king's *archimignon*, the Duke of Épernon. However, the subject of *favoritisme* did not become immediately a regular theatrical theme in France. Compared to Spain and England, in France the development of theater, in general, and the dramatization of favorites, in particular, occurred gradually and relatively late. At the turn of the seventeenth century, France was suffering a series of civil wars which, together with other factors such as poverty, insufficient communications, and difficulties for players, conditioned the growth of French theater (Lancaster 1.1: 13; Lough, *Paris Theatre Audiences* 7–44). One of the most prominent French playwrights, Pierre Corneille, began to produce his dramatic work in the 1630s and 1640s, and these are also the years in which the figure of the favorite became a prevalent character in the French stage, just when the topic of political favoritism began to decline in the theaters of Spain and England.

Court ballet

Although theater in France gained its great momentum in the 1630s, under the governance of Cardinal Richelieu, in the previous epoch there existed another type of performance which was also important for the representation of political favoritism: the *ballet de cour* or court ballet. Prior to the extraordinary development of theater, the court ballet and its combination of poetry, music, dance, and costumes constituted the prime dramatic entertainment in France and continued to be the main diversion for nobles and kings.

It is worth noting that although the portrayal of royal favorites in court ballet seems to be unique to French culture, the influence of this spectacle reached other European countries, especially England where Ben Jonson composed some masques based on his knowledge of the French art

(McGowan 232–45). Moreover, dancing was a highly valued skill in the extravagant courts of Europe, to the extent that English monarchs were accused of favoring dancers over statesmen (Perry, *Literature* 49). Favorite ministers like Lerma and Buckingham, apart from being accomplished dancers, strengthened their prestige and public image by sponsoring numerous and costly courtly dances such as masques and *saraos* (García García "Las fiestas de Corte").

In France, already in the 1580s, *Le Balet Comique de la Royne* (1581) starred one of Henri III's leading favorites, his *mignon* the Duke of Joyeuse. By 1620, court ballet was a well-defined dramatic genre that high-powered ministers used for their own propagandistic purposes. This was the case for the Duke of Luynes, a skillful dancer favored by the young King Louis XIII (1610–43) between 1617 and 1621. In these years, the figure of Luynes was exalted in several ballets resulting in what has been called "worship of the favorite" (Amstutz, *La Fable du favori* 440–52). Although these ballets staged ancient myths and medieval stories, their main goal was to project the contemporary political scene and social order at court. The fact that the court ballets were performed by the king, his relatives, his close friends, and his courtiers made the political messages of the performances still more evident (Downey).

Court ballet develops a geometric choreography in which each of the spaces where the dancers position themselves has a symbolic meaning (Van Orden). The choreography is led by the king, whom all the actors follow in a series of coordinated moves. This symbolic organization represents the control of the court by Louis XIII, who is the source of the fortune and wealth that courtiers pursue. The favorite of the king, the Duke of Luynes, stands out from all the other courtiers. Although Louis XIII plays the symbolic role of head of the political system, Luynes is the true protagonist of the ballet performance; he represents the perfect courtier and the ideal favorite. The favorite of Louis XIII always acts the part of the hero while the young king plays secondary roles. In the *Ballet d'Apollon* (1621), for example, Luynes impersonates the Greek god Apollo and Louis XIII appears as the chief blacksmith.

The death of Luynes in 1621 marked the end of these court ballets featuring royal favorites. Henceforth court ballet was still an artistic event used by the monarchy for propagandistic purposes, but its messages were presented in a more allegorical manner. Furthermore, in the following years court ballet experienced a process of theatricalization through which the importance of the acting was emphasized at the expense of the musical and poetic components of the ballet. This new mode of delivering political ideologies through court ballet was mastered by the quintessential favorite of Louis XIII, Armand-Jean du Plessis, better known as Cardinal and Duke of Richelieu. Richelieu incorporated court ballet into his patronage and made this spectacle even more political than had been earlier, but the focus of the performance moved from the character of the favorite to the monarchy of Louis XIII. As Giuliano Ferretti has studied, in court ballet Richelieu strengthened his authority as the king's prime minister by means of lauding the regime of Louis XIII (504–15). This regime was obviously orchestrated by Richelieu, who patronized the arts in France *in extenso*.

Ministère de Richelieu (1624–42)

The importance of Richelieu as patron of the arts in France is enormous. His contribution to the promotion of theater – the most relevant to this research – is close to that of painting and sculpture, the other great interests of the cardinal-duke.[1]

Richelieu was involved with the world of letters since his rise to power in the 1620s. As sole favorite of the king and supreme patron of cultural production, he extended his patronage to many writers who, in exchange for the protection and promotion of their works, celebrated the triumphs of his *ministère* and propagated a glorious image of Louis XIII's reign. Among these writers, in particular, one can find numerous dramatists given that the cardinal had a special fondness for theater. Indeed, Richelieu transformed the theater in France by way of promoting and supporting the practice of the dramatic art, and he was himself a playwright who authored, coauthored, censored, and reviewed plays. This artistic facet makes Richelieu an exceptional favorite. His wide patronage and his predilection for collecting art can be compared to those of the Duke of Buckingham or his counterpart the Duke of Lerma. However, no other European royal minister was as involved in dramatic poetry as was the French cardinal. Favorites, caring for their public image at court, used to approve or commission a dramatist to write a play praising their persona, but they were unable to compose dramas themselves. Richelieu went beyond this patronage activity and engaged himself in writing, reviewing, providing plots and outlines, and commenting on dramas.

One of the major achievements of Richelieu in the field of theater was the foundation of the Académie Française in 1635. This public institution, which was different from the literary academies sponsored by noblemen, helped financially to support the work of dramatists (Fumaroli, "Les intentions"). An annual funding provided by the Académie helped to make theater a regular activity independent from the diverse types of rewards that poets received from their *mécènes* or patrons. This sort of state patronage masterminded by Richelieu encouraged many writers to take interest in the Parisian court and made the career of playwriting "tolerably lucrative" (Lough, "The Earnings" 324). For a playwright, to penetrate the networks of influence that led to Richelieu became a strategy to gain status and economic stability. Pierre Corneille and Jean Rotrou, among many others, were subsidized by the *premier ministre*.

In addition, at a time when there existed only two permanent theaters in Paris (Hôtel de Bourgogne and Théâtre du Marais), Richelieu reserved a room in his Palais-Cardinal to stage dramatic performances. Here theater met with his passions for painting and sculpture. This artistic arrangement shows the new aesthetic of theater and performance that Richelieu encouraged by blending together dramatic poetry and stage decoration (Bayard 475). While that space of his palace was still hosting performances, Richelieu gave orders to build a more modern and spacious theater in a different room of the Palais-Cardinal known as the Grande Salle.[2] This new private theater was inaugurated in 1641 for the premiere of the play *Mirame*, by Jean Desmarets de Saint-Sorlin (1595–1676). Desmarets was first Chancellor of the Académie Française and worked as Richelieu's official dramatist for a few years. In fact, most scholars agree that Richelieu wrote or at least coauthored some of the plays attributed to Desmarets.

As for Richelieu's activity as a writer, he produced abundant work in prose, but it is rather difficult to determine his degree of participation in the composition of dramatic works. He never appeared as the author of a play, although it is known that he collaborated, sometimes extensively, in more than one. Two examples are *Mirame* and *Europe*, both originally attributed to Desmarets and launched, in 1641 and 1642, respectively, in the Grande Salle of the Palais-Cardinal. In the most recent edition of *Europe*, both Desmarets and Richelieu appear as authors of the dramatic text. As one could imagine, many of the dramas that Richelieu commissioned and in some cases coauthored were intended to convey political ideologies regarding his government. This was the case for *Europe*, an allegorical drama defending Richelieu's policies during The Thirty Years' War (Hall), and for *Mirame*, which condemns the love affair between the French Queen Anne of Austria, a political opponent of Richelieu, and the English favorite the Duke of Buckingham (Couton 51–78).

As with court ballet, Richelieu used theater as a political weapon to strengthen his position as the king's chief favorite, and he did so by means of propaganda in favor of the government that he controlled rather than by focusing on his individual persona. He defended his belief that theater was useful to the state and this idea can be seen, in addition to the plays on which the *cardinal-duc* directly put his hands, in the new type of theater that he promoted. Corneille, for instance, under Richelieu's influence, in the late 1630s and early 1640s wrote several Roman plays – e.g. *Horace*, dedicated to the Cardinal – to foster the idea of a modern state and nation. In those years, the subject of history played an important role in theater, but, as Andrea Frisch has argued, a current trend of *oubliance* or forgetfulness – which was common among both historians and dramatists – tended to reject the dramatization of French history, especially the recent wars of religion. Forgetting differences was a strategy for reconciliation in the campaign, orchestrated by Richelieu, to create and project the image of a centralizing and united monarchy under Louis XIII. From this perspective, the imperial Roman past, and more in particular the years of *Pax Augusta*, was a rather appropriate historical setting for the dramas performed after the Peace of

Alais (1629). In doing so, playwrights could present their contemporary political ideologies in a remote past, far from the most immediate decades of rebellions and bloody civil wars.

The play *Cinna* (1640), for instance, is understood within that context. This drama, like others by Corneille, shows a well-elaborated intrigue – Cinna's secret conspiracy against Augustus – combined with deep and even dense reflections on politics, so much so that, on occasions, it appears more as a political treatise than an entertaining drama. The end of the play, when Augustus defuses Cinna's conspiracy, is meant to be a glorification of the autocratic ruler, and this ruler is the French monarch rather than the Roman emperor. However, Corneille's political message goes beyond this exaltation of the monarch. *Cinna* portrays also a(n) (imperial) favorite (5.2.1620), who, thanks to the clemency of his superior, is not punished but rewarded. This presence of a favorite dramatic character was common in the era of Richelieu when political favoritism became a regular theatrical topic.

Drames des favoris

Throughout the first decades of the seventeenth century, French dramatists progressively put aside religious controversy to deal with political issues, and this route led gradually to the *mise en scène* of political favoritism on the French stage (Amstutz, *La Fable du favori* 361–452). As an example of this path, the tragic character of Haman, who, according to the *Book of Esther*, ascended to power by the Persian ruler Ahasuerus, was seen as a religious figure in early seventeenth-century French dramas and later on as a royal favorite, for instance in the play *Tragédie nouvelle de la perfidie d'Aman mignon et favori du Roy Assuerus*. This play was written around 1617, a year marked by the fall and murder of Concino Concini, the first chamberlain of Louis XIII and favorite of the regent Maria de' Medici (Dubost).[3] Henceforth, the Duke of Luynes, who was featured heavily in court ballet, served as favorite minister of the young Louis XIII for a short period of time. It was also around these years that the term *favori* entered French prose narrative (Amstutz, *La Fable du favori* 453) and some of the first dramas focusing on favorite characters were sporadically performed.

The appearance of favorites in theatrical performances became more regular throughout the 1630s and 1640s, coinciding with the *ministère* of Richelieu, the increase of Roman tragedies, and also a remarkable vogue for plays in the style of Spanish drama. As for this last trend, one of the most outstanding imitators was Jean de Rotrou, a dramatist protégé of Richelieu, who, in turn, might have also had a taste for *comedias*, since his library at the Palais-Cardinal held works by Spanish playwrights, among them Lope de Vega (Wollenberg 325; Tuilier 421).[4] Rotrou wrote at least six dramas featuring favorite ministers based on Spanish plays such as *El ejemplo mayor de la desdicha* (c. 1625), a *comedia de privanza* by Antonio Mira de Amescua (Bauer-Funke; Teulade). These dramas lost some of their original models by being adapted to the French dramatic structure of the time; this is the Aristotelian aesthetic that was promoted by the omnipresent Richelieu (Bayard 486).[5] Thus the plays were divided into five acts, lacked buffoon characters, and followed the classical canons of the unity of action, time, and place. Apart from Spanish drama, recent English history and theater also provided examples of royal favoritism that French playwrights brought on stage, for instance in the plays featuring favorites by Gautier de Costes de la Calprenède about the fall from favor of the Earl of Essex (1639) or Edward II of England (1640), in addition to a few dramas starring Sejanus, the renowned favorite dramatized by Ben Jonson (Amstutz, *La Fable du favori* 393–422).

The theatrical representations of favorites in France, however, deviate from the development of Spanish and English dramas on favorites in some important aspects. The French character of the favorite, besides owing some of his features to other dramatic models, overlaps often with the functions of other types of ministers or *conseillers* (Gethner, "Power Grabbing" 213; Amstutz, "Favoris et conseillers"). Although the favorite became a better-defined character during the governance of Cardinal Richelieu, especially in tragedies, it is rare to find French dramas of that period portraying all-powerful ministers in the same manner that the Spanish and English did. Principally, French playwrights focus on the intimate relationship between monarchs and ministers, but they rarely comment on the socio-political implications of favoritism such as the distribution of royal favor and the favorites' dominion over the courtly relations of patronage. In this regard, for example, the political issues that create a confrontation between the king and the favorite of Lope de Vega's *Don Lope de Cardona* (c. 1611) become, in Rotrou's version of this play (*Don Lope de Cardone*, 1652), issues of love (Teulade 111–2). In some plays, moreover, the favor of a ruler is shared with more than one favorite, for example in *Cinna*, in which the friendship of Maxime with the emperor almost equals that of the protagonist, or in *Clitandre* (1631), another play by Corneille, in which the stories of Rosidor, the king's favorite, and Clitandre, the prince's favorite – or *mignon*–, interweave.

At any rate, French theaters staged favorite ministers for roughly a century, from the plays that commented on Henri III's *mignons* in the 1580s, to the fall of Concini and rise to power of Luynes, in 1617, to the appearance of *Le Favori, ou la Coquette* in the second half of the seventeenth century. This mature and concise play, which in the last years has received considerable attention by scholars, is regarded to be the last and, in some ways, a synthesis of that trajectory of the favorite character in French drama.

Le Favori, ou la Coquette

Le Favori, ou la Coquette (1664)[6] has also the particularity of being, to my knowledge, the only drama on a favorite minister written by a female playwright, Marie-Catherine Desjardins, also known as Madame de Villedieu

(1640–83). Despite the large number of female writers in seventeenth-century France, theater was a genre dominated almost exclusively by men and Desjardins was the only woman who wrote history plays (Goldwyn, "Men in Love" 64–7). She gained fame as a writer and after a brief incursion into playwriting her name appeared along with that of Desmarets, Corneille, and Molière. *Le Favori*, which was her third play, was performed multiple times before the urban audience of Paris and even had the privilege to be staged before King Louis XIV and his court in the gardens of Versailles. This play was, however, Desjardins' last dramatic work. Regardless of the recognition of her work, her income as a playwright remained low and the royal pension that Hugues de Lionne, dedicatee of *Le Favori*, arranged for her arrived late (in 1676) and greatly reduced.[7]

Le Favori is a short drama – 1427 verses – about love and politics at court that features the figure of a royal favorite named Moncade. The play, which follows the rules of the three unities – action, time, and place–, is set in the fictitious kingdom of Barcelona, where an unnamed monarch rules, and most of the characters have Spanish names. The plot of *Le Favori* is simple. It opens with Moncade facing his dilemma: how to deal with his love for Lindamire while simultaneously fulfilling his duties as the king's favorite. This king, in an act of apparent jealousy and tyranny, imprisons Moncade under the pretext of being an inattentive minister, absorbed as he is by his love life. This chain of events, which happens in the first of five acts, opens the conflict of the play – the tragedy of Moncade – until it is resolved in the last scenes when the king of Barcelona restores the favorite minister to his original position.

This storyline might have been the plot of any of the many seventeenth-century dramas conveying obvious political messages in support of monarchs and their favorites. This type of drama is common, for example, in early modern Spanish theater, and in fact, scholars assume that Tirso de Molina's *El amor y el amistad*, a play dated to around 1620 and published in 1634, is the source of *Le Favori*. However, there are reasons to doubt whether there exists a direct relation between Desjardins' play and Tirso's *El amor y el amistad*, which seems to be both a reworking of and a model for other Spanish plays, and its story can be also found in Quevedo's *Grandes anales de quince días* of 1621 (Kennedy). Perry Gethner, who has studied *Le Favori* the most in relation to *El amor y el amistad*, admits with surprise that no previous scholar, aside from mentioning vague parallels, has extended the analogy between Tirso's and Desjardins' plays ("Power Grabbing" 218, n. 2). Moreover, as Gethner notes in his comparative study, there is a considerable number of differences between the two plays that distance Desjardins from her supposed source ("Love and Friendship").[8] This all indicates that the singularity of *El amor y el amistad* – which depicts the favorite of a count rather than a royal favorite – as the only source of *Le Favori* seems certainly questionable. There are other Spanish plays – e.g. *Cautela contra cautela*, by either Tirso de Molina or Mira de Amescua–, that tell similar stories, in substance, to that of *El amor y el amistad*, and the only name that Desjardins takes from Tirso's play is, arguably, Moncada (in French, Moncade), which appears in other *comedias. La paciencia en la fortuna*, for example, also features a royal favorite named Moncada who, like the protagonist of *Le Favori*, suffers stoically the arbitrary behavior of his monarch until the end, and yet, it seems almost impossible that Desjardins, whose familiarity with Spanish drama is unknown, could have remotely known this play.

In any case, regardless of the specific sources that could have inspired Desjardins, it is worth noting more carefully the Spanish setting and appearance of *Le Favori*. It is not a coincidence that a French play featuring a royal favorite uses a Spanish setting due to two main factors. First and foremost, the phenomenon of political favoritism was singularly strong in early modern Spain and its reputation was internationally known. Some playwrights in England also chose Spanish soil on which to stage royal favorites, for example in *Henry the Una(ble)* – the impotent – (c. 1619), which depicts Henry IV's favorite who is urged to procreate with the queen in fifteenth-century Castile (Steggle 119–32), or *The Great Favourite* (1668), an adaption of an earlier play titled *The Duke of Lerma* and featuring the Spanish favorite of Philip III (Shewring). In addition to the fame of Spanish favorites, Spanish *comedia* had a significant effect on the development of French drama, especially during the central decades of the seventeenth century (Marchal-Weyl). More particularly, as mentioned earlier, a considerable number of French dramas on favorites had certain Spanish *comedias de privanza* as models. In this regard, it is not surprising if one finds traces of Spanish dramas in *Le Favori* since Desjardins, regardless of her knowledge of any of those dramas, wrote her play on a topic that in France had been to a certain degree developed under the influence of Spanish *comedia*. Although scholars have mainly focused on the comparison of *Le Favori* to Tirso's *El amor y el amistad*, the parallels between Desjardins' dramatic work and Spanish plays are numerous. For instance, Amelia Sanz, as an exception to that scholarship, has studied Desjardins' plays in the light of Spanish *comedia* as a whole and her research suggests, among others, parallels between Desjardins and Lope de Vega and between *Le Favori* and *El burlador de Sevilla*.

In any case, *Le Favori* stands on its own and cannot be reduced to a typical – Spanish or not – play on favorites as it could appear, but this is a unique, meaningful, and ambiguous dramatic text offering multiple readings. First and foremost, it clearly shows, as few plays do, two mutually opposite ways of behaving at court. On the one hand, Moncade together with his beloved Lindamire would represent traditional noble values, such as loyalty and generosity, associated with the heroic characters of Corneille's theater. They repudiate the flattery and the hypocrisy currently dominant in court, and feeling discomfort, they refrain from favors and avoid the royal palace. Moncade, who is apprehensive about his own exclusive position as the king's chief minister, is tempted from the beginning to live alone in his country house. When the favorite is sentenced to exile, he and Lindamire can barely restrain their enthusiasm. For them, this circumstance opens the possibility to enjoy their pure love, as she says:

> "I thank you, exile, you remove my rival.
> Today I triumph; favor is no more.
> Moncade can henceforth give me all his heart.
> What innocent joys this exile shall prepare us!" (3.6.826–9)

On the other hand, Elvire and Clotaire are two egoistic and vain parasites who quickly forget their false love and friendship toward the fallen favorite. They represent the ambitious and morally degenerated courtiers who shamelessly pursue their own goals. Lindamire calls Clotaire "court chameleon" (3.3.712), a metaphor used by Lucas Gracián Dantisco in his manual of courtly conduct, *Galateo español* (50), to refer to those who change depending on the situation. The same term is used in a pejorative way in Lope de Vega's *Rimas* (2.245.173–6) as well as in the Spanish drama *Cómo ha de usarse del bien y ha de prevenirse el mal* by Payo, a Neostoic royal favorite adopting an attitude similar to that of Moncade and Lindamire: "those full of ambitions / are chameleons" (1.530–1).

Between these two ways of courtly behavior, one more ethical and the other more pragmatic, at the end the king appears to position himself next to Moncade and Lindamire and, what is more, condemns Clotaire, who suffers pangs of conscience, by saying of the latter:

> "He has well deserved such stinging self-reproach,
> And his example must serve as a sign to all
> That no one clearly views a monarch's heart,
> And that to get out of so great a danger,
> There is nothing like nobility of soul" (5.7.1419–23)

This final resolution and the king's endorsement of the values represented by Moncade, in contrast to the conduct of immoral courtiers, can be interpreted as a final triumph of the traditional, noble attitude of those gathering around the royal favorite. This is the conclusion that some scholars reach. For Perry Gethner, for example, the king of *Le Favori* shows himself to be a fair ruler and Desjardins suggests that the moral courtly degeneration is "limited to a small number of individuals who in any case are far removed from the real power" ("Love, Self-Love" 418). However, the play has also been approached from different angles. Delphine Amstutz addresses her attention to the protagonist and states that the innovation of *Le Favori* is that the playwright chooses Moncade's point of view, thus delving into the interiority, the psychological side of the royal favorite (*La Fable du favori* 365). This introspective analysis underlines the mental feebleness of Moncade, who suffers from *mélancolie* (1.6.261), something that seems to have also afflicted actual favorites like the Duke of Luynes and the Duke of Lerma. Examples of this mental condition can be also found in French and Spanish dramas on favorites such as Corneille's *Cinna* (3.2.858), Vélez de Guevara's *El espejo del mundo* (2.1596–653), and Mira de Amescua's *La adversa fortuna de don Álvaro de Luna* (3.2327, 2433). According to Renaissance theorists of courtly politics and conduct such as Machiavelli and Castiglione, melancholy is inappropriate for a favorite minister (Royé). Melancholy shows indifference and lack of care about government affairs, inhibits procedures and decision-makings requiring high agility, and casts doubts upon the monarch's choices. For all these reasons, the melancholic Moncade proves to be an unsatisfactory court favorite and the king's reaction, imprisoning his favorite, is not only justified but also, Jocelyn Royé thinks, proof of the apologetic nature of *Le Favori*, which presents a positive image of the monarchy.

From an opposite perspective, some scholars have remarked on the importance in *Le Favori* of the chameleon-like courtiers, and more in particular that of Elvire, *la coquette* of the play's subtitle (Sternberg-Greiner). Elvire loses her interest in Moncade upon his fall from grace and in the last words of the drama she expresses her pragmatism and thoughts on her new lover – named Lope – without remorse: "All this is not worth any conversation. / Don Lope's waiting; he's my consolation" (5.8.1426–7). In this regard, Elvire might be considered the true heroine of Desjardins' play, since her opportunism and ability to dissimulate make her a master of courtly life. From this point of view, Julian Killey has argued, Moncade's sincerity proves to be a failed strategy to survive at court and the weak *favori*, ironically treated by Desjardins, would simply be a "naïve dupe" (12), a comical figure tricked by the monarch.

Although *Le Favori* has been interpreted from several points of view, it has scarcely been analyzed within the wider framework of European early modern dramas on favorites and, more particularly, within the context of Neostoicism. This intellectual movement had a great impact in seventeenth-century France through the works of Justus Lipsius and those of Lipsian derivation such as Guillaume du Vair's *De la Constance et consolation ès calamitez publiques* (1595) and Pierre Charron's *De la Sagesse* (1601). All of these works contributed largely to shaping the political views of royal favorites such as Richelieu (Elliott, *Richelieu and Olivares* 24–7) and the dramatic work of playwrights such as Corneille (Maurens). As was the case in Spain, Neostoicism in France had Seneca as its main reference and it deviated as well to a Christianization of the Stoic principles (Carabin). Traces of this Neostoicism can be found throughout *Le Favori* and therefore a comparative analysis between this play and *La paciencia*, which portrays a Senecan favorite, is necessary in order to shed light on the multinational nature of dramas on favorites.

Some of the Stoic features that characterize Gastón de Moncada are also shared by the character Moncade, from *Le Favori*, a play that bears more than one resemblance to *La paciencia*. Gastón and Moncade, aside from having a similar family name associated with the north-east of Spain where their actions take place, are favorite ministers who enjoy solitude. The two favorites enjoy the retirement from the court in their country houses, which are the scenes where most action of both plays occurs. Like Gastón's estate, which is located in the remote countryside in Aragon, Moncade also owns a palace of extraordinary architecture and in complete harmony with nature, as Alvar describes it:

> "This grand variety of hilss and plains,
> These splendid gardens, marble statues, fountains,
> These sacred refuges of shade and awe,
> This fertile countryside..." (1.1.93–6)

In these privileged spaces, throughout the first act of each play and under similar circumstances, the conflicts of the plots develop. Members of the court, including the king and his close followers, visit the favorite on his properties. This visit interferes with the serenity that both Gastón and Moncade seek and plants the seeds of conflict with their monarch. Henceforth Moncade, like Gastón, suffers the punishment of a king who, at the end, acts justly and restores him to favor. Throughout this time, Moncade remains static and obeys the king's arbitrary decisions "without complaint or murmur" (2.5.546), showing also a stoic attitude that reminds us of Gastón.[9]

Nevertheless, the character of Moncade is different from that of Gastón in some important ways. Whereas Gastón is a virtuous favorite who unjustly suffers the tyranny of King Pedro, the disfavor of the king that Moncade experiences is more justifiable. As we learn from the first scene of *Le Favori*, the distance between Moncade and the king predates the compressed time frame of the play. Due to his depression, which is caused by his love for Lindamire, Moncade's coldness toward the king is already known by everyone at court when the story of *Le Favori* begins. Prior to this moment, the king, in order to rejoin his relationship with Moncade, showered him with "pleasures, feasts, favors, presents, honors, bounty" (1.1.78) without changing the favorite's attitude. What we see in the first act of *Le Favori* is the monarch's final attempt to fix his problems with Moncade. The king brings then the court, including Lindamire (the favorite's "ladylove" 1.1.84), to Moncade's country house to make him happy, but the favorite is immersed in his own thoughts and, except for Lindamire, he ignores the king and the rest of the court. This contempt nears a decisive moment when Moncade fails to meet with the king, who waits for his favorite in vain, to go hunting. The king's subsequent angry reaction seems logical in light of Moncade's lack of appreciation and interest in his responsibilities as the king's favorite. In fact, Moncade's attitude is inconceivable in a court society in which some of the greatest offices, such as the Lord Chamberlain and the first Gentleman of the Bedchamber, involve preparing the royal attire and shoes while the king wakes up (Elias, esp. 91–2).

Another significant difference between *La paciencia* and *Le Favori* is the role of Lindamire, whose virtues amend some of the flaws of Moncade as a royal favorite. Indeed, Lindamire is crucial in the course of the political events of *Le Favori* and this particularity distinguishes this play from other theatrical representations of favorite ministers. According to Henriette Goldwyn, Desjardins' history plays are characterized by a subordination of politics, the public field dominated by men, to love, which is the private sphere where women can exert their influence. This subordination implies the predominance of heroines over male characters who, regardless of their political positions, are portrayed as "men in love"; in other words, the dominance of the love theme results in "the emergence of a hero who is not only a conqueror but a respectful and tender lover" (Goldwyn, "Men in Love," 65). In *Le Favori*, the depiction of Moncade as both a reputed military[10] and romantic man fits into that category and puts forward for consideration the importance of his lover. However, compared to the attention received by Moncade and Elvire, the characters on which the discussion about the protagonists of *Le Favori* has been mainly focused, scholars have scarcely addressed the character of Lindamire and, even less, her importance in regard to royal favoritism which is, after all, the subject underlying the courtly intrigues of the play. In what follows, by focusing on the role of Lindamire, it will be argued that this character is key to understanding the particular position enjoyed by Moncade and, therefore, that she is the play's heroine as much as or more than the royal favorite is the hero.

That Lindamire plays a major role in *Le Favori* is clearly shown by the fact that she is the reason for which the king removes Moncade from power; furthermore, in turn, she also makes the monarch restore the favorite to his initial position. As we learn from Moncade, he and Lindamire have been romantically involved for two years (3.6.851), and although he aspires to marry her, she always finds excuses to delay their marriage. This situation changes as soon as Moncade is deprived of the king's favor. She then becomes interested in joining him because his life is no longer attached to the duties and public exposure of a royal favorite, which were the reasons why she had been reluctant to share her feelings with him. Once Moncade faces exile, the two lovers make plans to live together in a different estate, but then the king arrests Moncade and prevents the union. This move unleashes the fury of Lindamire, who decides to reveal her love for Moncade to the king. Finally, the monarch, convinced that this is true love, discharges his favorite and announces the wedding between Moncade and Lindamire. Throughout this time, which is basically the entire plot of the play, Moncade certainly proves to be unable to remedy his problems. It is Lindamire who creates his misfortunes and she is also the one who resolves them. Differently from dramas on favorites such as *La paciencia*, in which the favorite's virtues are finally rewarded by the monarch, in *Le Favori* it is Lindamire's true love and ability to speak convincingly which lead the monarch to find a favorable solution for his favorite. This situation makes Moncade's position dependent on Lindamire, and his flaws are compensated by her virtues.

Indeed, Lindamire shows some of the features that are associated with an accomplished courtier and, what is more, with an ideal favorite minister. As it is shown from the beginning of the play, she distrusts courtly life, but this does not disqualify her from being a capable courtier. Like Elvire, Lindamire knows how to dissimulate, as she is able to keep her real thoughts and feelings toward Moncade a secret. Speaking of Lindamire, Elvire says she is a "heart of steel" (4.5.1038) and her sudden feelings for Moncade are nothing but "skillfull masks to hide suspicious business" (4.5.1045). Although these are her rival's accusatory words, Lindamire is indeed pragmatic and avoids Moncade's speculations on whether he is loved for his personality or just for his high position. She clearly advises him to be happy, regardless of the reasons: "Provided one is happy, *I* maintain / That one can dispense with asking for the reason" (1.4.239–40). From these words, one can infer that Lindamire's approach to love is no less opportunistic than Elvire's, since she would not worry about the motives behind an amorous relationship as long as it made her happy. In her case, fortunately for her, Lindamire achieves her union with Moncade as the sole royal favorite, thus enjoying Moncade's person and position. These two sides of Moncade's life seem to be equally important to her, as she admits in one of the last scenes of the play (5.4.1242–59). More importantly, for Lindamire those thoughts belong to one's private life and should not interfere with public affairs. This is why Moncade fails to be a proper favorite minister, because his *mélancolie* affects his political responsibilities,[11] and at the same time, that is also why Lindamire is upset with the king, because he meddles in his favorite's personal life. She says:

> "Till now I did not know that royal power
> Had legal right to make a heart its slave.
> I knew our duty was to fear and obey,
> But as for the liberty to love and hate,
> I thought kings left that to individuals" (3.1.617–21)

As one can see, Lindamire has advice and criticisms for everybody, including the king, which is an indication of how dominant her wisdom and motivations are in the play. In her first appearance, early in the morning when the courtiers are still inside, Lindamire is on a balcony reading verses concerning an idyllic symbiosis between nature and love (1.4).[12] This is a routine that she repeats every morning (1.4.191–2) and that contrasts, as Lindamire remarks, with Moncade's ignorance of the countryside's "pleasures" (1.4.202) and his more general disdain for nature, as he admits: "To see the sun rise matters little to me" (1.4.207). Contrary to the virtuous Neostoic favorites, such as Gastón de Moncada, who cultivate their wisdom in harmony with nature, Moncade spends time in his country residences but does not have that same connection with the natural world. It is the wise Lindamire who, unlike Moncade, exalts the *beatus ille* and practices Neostoic virtues such as constancy and patience. In his relationship with Lindamire, Moncade is an impatient lover ("she checks my impatience")[13] who cannot control his passion, which results in failing to properly act as the king's favorite. On the contrary, Lindamire's exceptional ability to check her amorous feelings makes her an "unfortunate slave of an austere virtue" (3.2.656). While Moncade leaves his political and romantic situation in the hands of the inconstant fortune (2.2.461–96), Lindamire shows an extraordinary constancy and determination to resolve the conflict throughout the play, especially toward the end when Moncade barely takes part in the course of events (he disappears in the fourth act). In the third act, Lindamire declares her love to Moncade and provides hope by undervaluing the scope of fortune, since the preciousness of their love is stronger than "fortune, hard as it may try."[14] In that same act Lindamire also confronts the immoral courtiers Clotaire, who seeks Moncade's ruin, and Elvire, who later mocks constancy as "a silly fancy dressed as a virtue."[15]

At the beginning of the fifth and final act, Lindamire feels that her "constancy must yield" (5.1.1157) because Moncade has been arrested. Apparently, nothing else can be done to free Moncade and Alvar encourages Lindamire to flee, since she would be also punished for loving a "guilty man" (5.1.1173). Yet Lindamire, in the face of adversity, decides to proceed calmly: "I shall await it all serenely" (5.1.1171), thus showing an attitude that recalls the stoicism of Gastón de Moncada more than the unrestraint of his wife Violante. Lindamire concludes her conversation with Alvar with a sentence that is Stoic through and through: "When hope is gone, there's nothing left to fear" (5.1.1217), which evokes a verse of Seneca's *Medea*: "Qui nil potest sperare, desperet nihil."[16]

This conversation between Lindamire and the servant Alvar is reminiscent of *La paciencia* when, also in the first scene of the last act, Gastón tells his servant Pantoja about his *desengaño* (36). Both in *Le Favori* and in *La paciencia* despair and disillusionment are followed by a sudden change in the character of the monarch, who, as the *deus ex machina*, puts an end to the conflict. Until that moment, Lindamire assumes some of the proper characteristics, such as constancy and patience, of an ideal Stoic favorite like Gastón. Moreover, in the last act of the play the king treats Lindamire "as equal to Moncade," she strives "to imitate him well" (5.2.1197–9), and speaks on behalf of Moncade "like an alter ego" (5.4.1317).

This convergence between Lindamire and the role of the royal favorite can be also seen in the participation and the dramatic function of her character within the tragicomic structure of *Le Favori*. Her participation in the play (24% of the lines spoken) almost equals that of Moncade (26%). If we divide this participation into acts, we realize that the royal favorite's appearance is concentrated mainly in the beginning (300 lines in the first two acts in contrast to 25 lines in the last two acts), whereas Lindamire barely appears at the beginning (37 lines in the first two acts) and takes an active part toward the end (112 lines in the last act). In accordance with what has been previously argued, these statistics show that while Moncade is obviously protagonist in the origin of the play's conflict – the problems between the monarch and his favorite–, Lindamire is more important in the resolution of that conflict. Furthermore, it is also significant that in a drama concerning a royal favorite Lindamire speaks in the only two soliloquies of *Le Favori*, which are strategically placed in a central position in the third act, more precisely before she confronts the enemies Clotaire and Elvire (3.2.649–62) and before she declares her love to Moncade (3.5.779–83).[17] By way of comparison, *La paciencia* includes only a soliloquy, which is also placed in the middle of the story,[18] albeit it is given to the favorite character. Finally, as Jocelyn Royé notes, above all the characters of *Le Favori* it is Lindamire who provides this play with a tragic dimension due to her integrity, virtuosity, and willingness to sacrifice (167).

In addition to her virtues and her determined participation in the development of the plot, there is another aspect of the character Lindamire that might accentuate her importance in *Le Favori*, and that is her own political position. Although Desjardins is ambiguous in stating it, there are reasons to believe that Lindamire is the king's daughter. This hypothesis is briefly noted by Gethner, who suggests that she could be the king's adoptive child ("Power Grabbing" 212). The most explicit verses to support this thesis are placed at the end of the play when the monarch says of Lindamire: "For whom I am less king than father, And whom I've taken care of since her birth" (5.5.1325–6). Amstutz, in her edition of *Le Favori*, compares this passage to that of Corneille's *Cinna* in which Emperor Augustus regards Émilie, the favorite's lover, as his daughter. However, while in *Cinna* it is clear that Émilie is not the emperor's natural daughter, since Augustus killed her father, the doubts about the relationship between the king of Barcelona and Lindamire remain in *Le Favori*. The comparison between Émilie and Lindamire would be more plausible if the latter "is an orphaned noblewoman who has been adopted by the king," as Gethner believes ("Fictional Women" 111). More importantly, that comparison properly highlights the influential role of both female characters and suggests a more general relation of *Le Favori* to *Cinna*. Indeed, the stories of these two plays bear some significant resemblances. Like Moncade, Cinna's problems with Augustus are motivated by his melancholy and love for Émilie, who, like Lindamire, shows a rebellious attitude toward the ruler. One of the last scenes of *Le Favori*, when Lindamire assumes responsibilities before the king for the crime for which Moncade has been punished and the latter attempts to protect her: "Ah, don't believe her, sir, this is pretense" (5.6.1353), reminds us of one of *Cinna*'s final scenes in which Émilie confesses her leading role in the conspiracy against Augustus and Cinna tells the emperor: "If she conspired, it was my doing. I, / I am the only autor of her crime" (5.1637–8).[19] The ending of both plays is similar, with the ruler forgiving the favorite and approving his relationship with his lover.

That Lindamire has a special relationship with the king, and, therefore, that she can effectively influence him, is remarked on by Moncade: "Knowing what power she has over your heart" (5.6.1354). This strong connection, possibly kinship, between Lindamire and the king would further explain the latter's need to test the nature of Moncade and Lindamire's relationship. By reacting angrily to the union of his favorite with Lindamire, the king would not simply be protecting his loved one, but more importantly, in political terms, he would be avoiding a usurpation of power. This preoccupation is manifest when the king asks Moncade: "How did you manage to seduce such a person [Lindamire]? / Was in it hopes that you'd usurp my crown?" (5.6.1360–1), and also when Moncade, unaware of Lindamire's feelings and skeptical about her delays to marry him, suspects that she is waiting to become queen along with Clotaire, who is a dethroned monarch of a neighboring and warring kingdom and who has been granted asylum in Barcelona:

> "She waits and waits for our armies to triumph.
> The name of queen contains so many charms
> That if Clotaire's restored to his estates,
> She'll shortly lose all memory of my suit" (1.3.173–6)

Lindamire must play a powerful role in the politics of Barcelona's kingdom in order to be considered, as Moncade depicts her, a potential queen. An indication of her power is given when her plans to go into voluntary exile together with Moncade are revealed. Moncade will be exiled to his own estate which, in turn, belongs to a province where Lindamire's "power almost equals the King's" (4.4.1005). Thus Lindamire plans to join Moncade in a province that, it is warned, once belonged to her family and, therefore, constitutes a threat to the kingdom (4.4.1004–7). Given the threat of a union between Moncade – who is after all a respected and influential courtier (3.1.632; 5.5.1322–3) – and Lindamire in a province supporting her over the king, the monarch, as soon as he learns their plans, imprisons Moncade and prevents Lindamire from joining forces with the favorite minister. In the end, however, the king gives in to Lindamire's wishes, for, as he says, she "makes my rights yield to those of her love" (5.5.1327).

As noted by Henriette Goldwyn, the description of that province favorable to Lindamire seems to be a reference to the Fronde, a series of mid-seventeenth-century wars defying King Louis XIV and involving distinguished aristocrats such as the Duchess of Montpensier – known as the Grande Mademoiselle – who was King Louis XIV's cousin and Desjardins' patron.[20] The fact that Moncade has brought peace to the kingdom of Barcelona for the last ten years, as Lindamire states (3.1.628), might be another reference to the Fronde, which ended about ten years before the composition of *Le Favori*. Furthermore, the Grande Mademoiselle could have been an inspiration for the character of Lindamire. This last hypothesis is briefly posited by Aurore Evain, who says that Lindamire reminds us of the rebellious women of the Fronde ("anciennes frondeuses"), particularly the Grande Mademoiselle, and that she "represents a counter-power so threatening that she refuses to give herself over to Moncade given that she is in conflict with the king's favor."[21] This pivotal role that Evain assigns to Lindamire is certainly in agreement with the figure of Anne Marie Louise d'Orleans, the Grande Mademoiselle, whose life and significance at the court of Louis XIV have been extensively studied.[22] Numerous aspects of the biography of this princess, called daughter of France, give force to this hypothesis.

Mademoiselle was born in 1627 at the Louvre and raised at the Tuileries Palace. She was the granddaughter of King Henri IV and the daughter of Gaston d'Orleans, the brother of King Louis XIII. This extraordinary genealogy along with her immense wealth made her a unique marital candidate in France and also in Europe, and in fact the affairs concerning her marriage were always of great importance at the French court. Mademoiselle, however, was independent enough to refuse the proposals of several candidates including the future Charles II of England, who lived in exile in France. Her rebellious attitude was clearly shown when she became a leader of the Fronde against her younger first cousin, King Louis XIV. She was then forced to live in exile for five years, a period in which she developed her interests in literature and drama as well as certain animadversion on life at court. Soon after she returned to court in 1657, she retired again, this time voluntarily, in order to pursue her literary motivations. Her correspondence of these years, which has been edited and studied by Joan DeJean, indicates that toward 1660 Mademoiselle wanted for herself a life retired from court and in harmony with nature to cultivate "everything that the wise men of antiquity held in esteem" (17). She imagined a community called "Republic," a "project of a solitary way of life for individuals who would agree to leave the court" (12–3), which became a utopian vision for unmarried women.

Louis XIV, with the aim of gaining control over the lands belonging to Mademoiselle, proposed to her new marital matches without being able to persuade her. These refusals moved the king to force her into a new exile from 1662 to 1664, the year in which she returned to court and Desjardins' *Le Favori* was first performed in Paris. At that moment, Mademoiselle had fallen in love with a rising courtly figure, the Duke of Lauzun, who throughout the 1660s "belonged to the small group of courtiers who surrounded Louis XIV in his pursuit of private pleasures" (Pitts, *La Grande Mademoiselle* 177). Lauzun and Mademoiselle saw each other on several occasions starting in 1659 when she was first captivated by him. However, the advancement of their relationship was continuously interrupted by the king's decisions. She remained far from both the court and Lauzun between 1662 and 1664, and in this last year Lauzun was imprisoned for six months. The reason of his imprisonment was seemingly an arbitrary decision of the king, who saw in Lauzun a rival competing for the same women pursued by the monarch. This episode had no apparent consequences for the relationship between the king and Lauzun, who remained being favored within the inner circle of the monarch. However, Lauzun was again arrested in 1671, soon after the king had approved his marriage with Mademoiselle (Pitts, *La Grande Mademoiselle* 177–212).[23]

This troubled relationship between a princess and a favorite of the king has resonance with the plot of *Le Favori*, especially with regard to the character of Lindamire and the significance of her marriage in the royal court. In *Le Favori*, Lindamire, like Mademoiselle, is also an influential woman, perhaps a princess, in the kingdom of Barcelona. Her power equals that of the king in the province where her family has been traditionally supported and her marital situation is of great importance to the king. In addition to her political position, other aspects of Mademoiselle's life resonate with the depiction of Lindamire as well. Philippe Amiguet portrays Mademoiselle as a pure and honest woman who had no interest in brief romantic relationships: "She was horrified by gallantry!" (336), which is certainly reminiscent of Lindamire's opposition to the fashionable courtly ethic of gallantry as exemplified by the character Elvire. In turn, Mademoiselle enjoyed spending time away from the royal court and cultivating her literary interests, like Lindamire did every morning when she read verses in an isolated spot.

In addition, Mademoiselle's love for Lauzun and the imprisonment of the latter in 1664 due to the king's arbitrariness are contemporary with the *mise en scène* of *Le Favori*. Desjardins would then be aware of Mademoiselle's feelings and state of mind. They had met around 1660 and since then they developed a close and lasting friendship. In 1663 Desjardins visited Mademoiselle in her exile while they were also engaged in written correspondence. This relationship involved Mademoiselle's patronage to Desjardins, who dedicated *Manlius* (1662) and *Lisandre* (1663) to her patron (Garapon 275–6). *Le Favori* was published in 1665 and dedicated to Desjardins' new patron, the prominent state minister Hugues de Lionne.[24] Although Desjardins' friendship with Mademoiselle lasted until at least 1680 when the latter agreed to be the godmother of Desjardins' son, Mademoiselle's patronage activities decreased throughout the 1660s and, consequently, she ceased to receive dedications (Garapon 277). When Desjardins decided to write *Le Favori* (1664), nonetheless, her patronage relationship with Mademoiselle was either still active or very fresh in mind; in any case, her friend Mademoiselle was likely an inspiration for Lindamire and perhaps, given the importance of this character, for the whole of story of the play.

In summary, Lindamire's role in *Le Favori* is paramount for several reasons. First, her feelings toward Moncade initiate and end, all at once, the beginning and end of the play's plot. Second, her participation in the restoration of the royal favorite is of great importance, especially since she adopts features that Moncade does not possess. Some of her Stoic virtues, such as patience and constancy, empower her to overcome adversity, which makes her not only a proficient courtier but also an ideal favorite minister. Finally, her high-powered position at court, possibly as kin of the monarch, makes her a key figure in the politics of the French court. Based on this importance of Lindamire, one can argue that if *Le Favori* tells the story of a king who becomes reconciled with his royal favorite, which is to a great extent the story of numerous dramas on favorites such as *La paciencia* and *Cinna*, at the same time this play features a wise, virtuous, and influential woman, Lindamire, who is able to raise controversies and intrigues in the palace as well as to successfully achieve her goals by persuading other characters, among them, mainly, the king and his chief minister.

Despite the importance of Lindamire and the values that she represents, *Le Favori*, nevertheless, presents a discussion about the principles of Neostoicism at large. Unlike *La paciencia*, in which the Neostoicism of the royal favorite finds almost no opposition and clearly triumphs as a model of conduct at court, in *Le Favori* the audience views a larger struggle between two models of court behavior. Although Lindamire plays a leading role among the group of moral characters upholding noble virtues such as courage and constancy, in *Le Favori* these traditional values are seriously called into question by the appearance and notability of the opportunistic and amoral characters of Clotaire and, principally, Elvire. This counterbalance between two opposing ways of life reflects the tensions within the French court society during the time in which the play was written. At that moment, after decades of extraordinary influence, objections to the principles of Neostoicism and particularly to Seneca's moral philosophy were frequent (Chariatte) at the same time that newer court figures, such as the coquette Elvire, became harbingers of the typical libertine characters of the eighteenth century (Goldwyn, "Mme de Villedieu" 115–6). Despite these critiques against Neostoicism, *Le Favori*, like *La paciencia*, associates the non-tragic royal favorite with Senecan virtues. In Jonson's *Sejanus His Fall*, in contrast, these virtues characterize the opposition to the evil and tragic favorite minister.

Notes

1 See Chancellerie, Mousnier and Mesnard, Mousnier, Boyer et al., especially the articles pertaining to theater, and Couton.

2 Contemporary descriptions and illustrations of this theater can be seen in Howarth 142–9.

3 Concini's downfall, as Bouteille-Meister studies, was staged in various plays.

4 On the influence of Lope's dramatic art on French drama, see Lombardi.

5 In comparison to French theater, the classical rules of drama barely left a mark on the Spanish and English dramas of the seventeenth century (Lough, "Drama and Society" 257–8).
6 All references to this play, henceforth referred to as *Le favori*, are to Delphine Amstutz's edition. For the translations into English, I follow Gethner's version of the play.
7 See Gethner's introduction to his edition of *Le Favori* and Goldwyn, "Les stratégies," esp. 31.
8 In the most recent edition of *Le Favori*, Delphine Amstutz claims also that *El amor y el amistad* is the source of inspiration for Desjardins and even includes parts of Tirso's play translated into French as an appendix. However, based on Gethner's remarks, Amstutz has more to say about the differences between the two plays than about their similarities ("Introduction," esp. 12–6). Amstutz, in turn, draws attention to the parallels between *Le Favori* and "la littérature galante" such as the novel *Clélie* by Madeleine de Scudéry, which recounts the love story between Princess Lindamire and the favorite Thémiste (32–44).
9 See, for instance, 2.2.473–83, and Amstutz's comments on Moncade's Neostoicism in the footnote.
10 See, for instance, what Lindamire says of Moncade to the king: "By making him gain numerous victories, / By giving honor to his glorious exploits," "I've seen him as a conqueror without rashness" (5.3.1245–6 and 56).
11 This is the argument developed by Jocelyn Royé, who underlines that Moncade confuses his love for Lindamire with his political position at court.
12 Gethner notes the exceptionality of this scene showing a female character reading on stage ("L'intériorité" 123). Amstutz, in her edition of *Le Favori* (p. 71, n. 34), offers several hypotheses regarding the source of those verses. Prominent among them is Boisrobert's *Coups d'amour et de fortune* (1656), a play set in Barcelona and featuring Roger de Moncade, as well as a reworking of Calderón de la Barca's *Lances de amor y fortuna* (Marchal-Weyl).
13 "elle oppose à mon impatience" (1.3.170).
14 "la fortune avec tous ses efforts" (3.6.803).
15 "une chimere habillée en vertu" (4.2.904).
16 Quoted by Amstutz in *Le Favori*, p. 137, note 113.
17 On the soliloquies in Desjardins' dramas, see Gethner, "L'intériorité." Gethner notes that *Le Favori* includes three "mini-monologues" ("passages where a character is alone briefly after their interlocutor's exit and gives a reply that is too short to indicate a new scene") by Moncade (121).
18 In the manuscript copy of the Biblioteca Nacional de España (26v); in the Parma manuscript, however, this soliloquy is placed toward the beginning of the third act (39).
19 Translated by John Cairncross, Penguin, 1975.
20 See Goldwyn's edition of *Le Favori*, p. 445, n. 37. On the Fronde, see Ranum.
21 "représente un contre-pouvoir d'autant plus menaçant qu'elle-même refuse de se donner à Moncade tant qu'elle est en concurrence avec la faveur du roi" (158).
22 See the works of Amiguet, Pitts (*La Grande Mademoiselle*), DeJean, and Garapon.
23 In prison, Lauzun joined Nicolas Fouquet who, upon Mazarin's death in 1661, aspired to be the new king's favorite. However, Fouquet was arrested that same year and died in jail in 1680 (Fumaroli, "Nicolas Fouquet;" Pitts, *Embezzlement*). When analyzing the historical context of *Le Favori*, scholars unanimously associate this play with Fouquet's arrest (see esp. Hogg and Evain), although this *lecture à clefs* has been recently questioned (Amstutz, "Introduction," esp. 22–3).
24 On the dedications and dedicatees of *Manlius* and *Le Favori*, see Goldwyn, "Les strategies."

Works Cited

Amiguet, Philippe. *Une princesse à l'école du Cid: La Grande Mademoiselle et son siècle, d'après ses mémoires*. A. Michel, 1957.

Amstutz, Delphine. "Favoris et conseillers sur là scene tragique du premier XVIIe siècle." *Dramaturgies du conseil et de la délibération*, edited by Xavier Bonnier and Ariane Ferry, CÉRÉdI, Actes de colloques et journées d'étude, no. 16, 2016, pp. 1–9, accessed 20 March, 2020, http://ceredi.labos.univ-rouen.fr/public/?favoris-et-conseillers-sur-la.html

———. "Introduction." Desjardins, *Le Favori*, pp. 5–44.

———. *La Fable du favori dans la littérature française du premier XVIIe siècle*. Dissertation, Université Paris-Sorbonne, 2013.

Bauer-Funke, Cerstin. "Análisis comparado de *El ejemplo mayor de la desdicha* de Antonio Mira de Amescua y *Bélisaire* de Jean Rotrou." *Actas del V Congreso Internacional de la Asociación Internacional Siglo de Oro (AISO)*, edited by Christoph Strosetzki, Iberoamericana, 2001, pp. 176–86.

Bayard, Marc. "Richelieu en scène, Buffequin en coulisse." Boyer et al., pp. 475–500.

Bouteille-Meister, Charlotte. "Interpréter l'événement pour le contrôler au début du règne personnel de Louis XIII. La mise en scène de l'actualité sur le théâtre: entre construction et célébration de l'action monarchique." *Interpreting in/of the Seventeenth Century*, edited by P. Zoberman, Cambridge Scholars Publishing, 2015, pp. 267–281.

Boyer, Jean-Claude et al., editors. *Richelieu patron des arts*. Maison des sciences de l'homme, 2009.

Carabin, Denise. *Les idées stoïciennes dans la littérature morale des XVIe et XVIIe siècles (1575–1642)*. H. Champion, 2004.

Chancellerie des Universités de Paris et Académie Française. *Richelieu et le monde de l'esprit*. Imprimerie Nationale, 1985.

Chariatte, Isabelle. "Le frontispice des *Réflexions ou sentences et maximes morales* de la Rochefoucauld: une clé de lecture à plusieurs niveaux." *Revue d'histoire littéraire de la France*, vol. 102, no. 4, 2002, pp. 637–43.

Cómo ha de usarse del bien y ha de prevenirse el mal. Edited by Paola Laskaris, Mauro Baroni, 2008.

Corneille, Pierre. *Cinna*. Edited by Alain Riffaud, Droz, 2011.

———. *Clitandre ou l'Innocence délivrée. Œuvres Complètes*. Vol. 1, edited by Georges Couton, Gallimard, 1980, pp. 91–173.

Couton, Georges. *Richelieu et le théâtre*. 1986. Eurédit, 2008.

DeJean, Joan. "Introduction: La Grande Mademoiselle." *Against Marriage: the Correspondence of La Grande Mademoiselle*. U of Chicago P, 2002, pp. 3–25.

Desjardins, Marie-Catherine (Madame de Villedieu). *Le Favori*. Edited by Delphine Amstutz, Hermann, 2017.

———. *Le Favori*. Edited by Henriette Goldwyn. *Théâtre de femmes de l'Ancien régime. XVIIe siècle*, edited by Aurore Evain et al., Publications de l'Université de Saint-Étienne, 2008, pp. 395–465.

———. *The Favorite Minister. The lunatic lover and other plays by French women of the 17th and 18th centuries*, edited by Perry Gethner, Heinemann, 1994, pp. 39–88.

Desmarets, Jean. *Mirame: Tragi-comédie*. Edited by Catherine Guillot and Colette Scherer, Presses Universitaires de Rennes, 2010.

Desmarets, Jean, and Armand du Plessis (Cardinal de Richelieu). *Europe: Comédie Héroïque*. Edited by Sylvie Taussig, Brepols, 2006.

Downey, Charles. "The Noble Participants in the Ballet of *La Délivrance de Renaud*." Garden, pp. 7–13.

Dubost, Jean-François. "Between *Mignons* and Principal Ministers: Concini, 1610–1617." Elliott and Brockliss, pp. 71–78.

El burlador de Sevilla (attributed to Tirso de Molina). 18th ed. Edited by A. Rodríguez, Cátedra, 2010.

Elias, Norbert. *La sociedad cortesana*. 1969. 2nd ed. Fondo de Cultura Económica, 2012.

Elliott, John. *Richelieu and Olivares*. Cambridge UP, 1984.

Elliott, John, and Laurence Brockliss, editors. *The World of the Favourite*. Yale UP, 1999.

Evain, Aurore. "Performance du *Favori* de Mme de Villedieu." Grande and Keller-Rahbé, pp. 147–59.

Ferretti, Giuliano. "La musique de Richelieu." Boyer et al., pp. 501–18.

Frisch, Andrea. *Forgetting Differences: Tragedy, Historiography, and the French Wars of Religion*. Oxford UP, 2015.

Fumaroli, Marc. "Les intentions de Richelieu, protecteur de l'Académie française." Mousnier, pp. 69–78.

———. "Nicolas Fouquet, the Favourite *Manqué*." Elliott and Brockliss, pp. 239–55.

Garapon, Jean. *La culture d'une princesse: Écriture et autoportrait dans l'œuvre de la Grande Mademoiselle (1627–1693)*. Honoré Champion, 2003.

García García, Bernardo José. "Las fiestas de Corte en los espacios del valido: la privanza del Duque de Lerma." *La fiesta cortesana en la época de los Austrias*, edited by García and María Luisa Lobato, Junta de Castilla y León, 2003, pp. 35–77.

Gethner, Perry. "Fictional Women Travelers in Plays by Women: Victims or Good Role Models?" *Women in French Studies*, vol. 7, 2018, pp. 106–119.

———. "L'intériorité dans le théâtre de Villedieu: monologues, réflexions, auto-analyse." Grande and Keller-Rahbé, pp. 119–30.

———. "Love and Friendship: From Tirso to Desjardins." *Papers on French seventeenth century literature*, vol. 32, no. 62, 2005, pp. 113–24.

———. "Love, Self-Love and the Court in *Le Favori*." *L'image du Souverain dans le théâtre de 1600 à 1650, Maximes, Madame de Villedieu: Actes de Wake Forest*, edited by Milorad Margitić and Byron Wells, Papers on French Seventeenth Century Literature, 1987, pp. 408–20.

———. "Power Grabbing and Court Opportunism: From Spain to France." *Echoes and Inscriptions: Comparative Approaches to Early Modern Spanish Literatures*, edited by Barbara Simerka and Christopher Weimer, Bucknell UP, 2000, pp. 120–8.

Goldwyn, Henriette. "Les stratégies de puovoir dans le paratexte de l'écriture théâtrale de Mme de Villedieu." Grande and Keller-Rahbé, pp. 29–41.

———. "Men in Love in the Plays of Mme de Villedieu." Lalande, pp. 64–83.

———. "Mme de Villedieu — La Transformation théâtrale: de l'héroïsme à l'épicurisme galant." *Cahiers du dix-septième*, vol. 11, no. 1, 2006, pp. 107–20.

Gracián Dantisco, Lucas. *Galateo Español*. 1582. Edited by Margherita Morreale, Consejo Superior de Investigaciones Científicas, 1968.

Grande, Nathalie, and Edwige Keller-Rahbé, editors. *Madame de Villedieu et le théâtre*, Narr, 2009.

Hall, H. Gaston. "'Europe', allégorie théâtrale de propagande politique." Mousnier and Mesnard, pp. 319–27.

Hogg, Chloé. "Staging Foucquet: Historical and Theatrical Contexts of Villedieu's *Le Favori*." Lalalande, pp. 43–63.

Howarth, William D., editor. *French Theatre in the Neo-classical Era, 1550–1789.* Cambridge UP, 1997.

Jonson, Ben. *Sejanus His Fall.* Edited by Tom Cain. *The Cambridge Edition of the Works of Ben Jonson*, 7 vols., edited by D. Bevington et al., Cambridge UP, 2012, vol. 2, pp. 195–391.

Kennedy, Ruth. "Notes on Two Interrelated Plays of Tirso: *El amor y el amistad* and *Ventura te dé Dios, hijo.*" *Hispanic Review*, vol. 28, no. 3, 1960, pp. 189–214.

Killey, Julian. *Desjardins'* Le Favori *and Moliere's* Tartuffe*: Dissimulators and dupes.* Thesis, U of North Carolina at Chapel Hill, 2010.

Lalande, Roxanne, editor. *A Labor of Love: Critical Reflections on the Writings of Marie-Catherine Desjardins (Mme de Villedieu).* Fairleigh Dickinson UP, 2000.

La paciencia en la fortuna. 1615. MS 16459. Biblioteca Nacional de España, Madrid. 1–56v.

La paciencia en la fortuna. CC*IV 28033, *Comedias de Diferentes Autores*, vol. 74, no. 2. Biblioteca Palatina di Parma, Parma. 1–55r.

Lancaster, Henry. *A History of French Dramatic Literature in the Seventeenth Century.* Johns Hopkins P, 1929–1942. 9 vols.

Lombardi, Marco. "Per impronte e indizi. Alcune tracce di Lope nella letteratura francese: norma e transgressione. La miscidanza dei generi. Lo spettatore. Il pubblico." Poggi and Profeti, pp. 303–19.

Lough, John. "Drama and Society." *The New Cambridge Modern History*, vol. 4, edited by J. P. Cooper, Cambridge UP, 1970, pp. 239–59.

———. *Paris Theatre Audiences in the Seventeenth & Eighteenth Centuries.* Oxford UP, 1957.

———. "The Earnings of Playwrights in Seventeenth-Century France." *The Modern Language Review*, vol. 42, no. 3, 1947, pp. 321–36.

Marchal-Weyl, Catherine. *Le tailleur et le fripier: Transformations des personnages de la comedia sur la scene francaise (1630–1660).* Droz, 2007.

Maurens, Jacques. *La tragédie sans tragique: Le néo-stoïcisme dans l'oeuvre de Pierre Corneille.* Armand Colin, 1966.

McGowan, Margaret M. *L'art du ballet de cour en France, 1581–1643.* Éditions du Centre national de la recherche scientifique, 1963.

Mira de Amescua, Antonio. *El ejemplo mayor de la desdicha.* Edited by M. Grazia Profeti. *Teatro completo.* Vol. 1, edited by A. de la Granja, Universidad de Granada, 2001, pp. 207–302.

Molina, Tirso de. Cómo han de ser los amigos *y* El amor y el amistad *(dos comedias palatinas).* Edited by María Teresa Otal, Instituto de Estudios Tirsianos, 2007.

Mousnier, Roland, editor. *Richelieu et la culture: Actes cu colloque international en Sorbonne.* Editions du Centre National de la Recherche Scientifique, 1987.

Mousnier, Roland, and Jean Mesnard, editors. *L'âge d'or du mécénat (1598–1661): Actes du colloque international CNRS.* Éditions du Centre National de la Recherche Scientifique, 1985.

Perry, Curtis. *Literature and Favoritism in Early Modern England.* Cambridge UP, 2006.

Pitts, Vincent. *Embezzlement and High Treason in Louis XIV's France: The Trial of Nicolas Fouquet*. Johns Hopkins UP, 2015.

———. *La Grande Mademoiselle at the Court of France: 1627–1693*. Johns Hopkins UP, 2000.

Ranum, Orest. *The Fronde: A French Revolution, 1648–1652*. W.W. Norton, 1993.

Royé, Jocelyn. "*Le Favori* ou la politique du coeur au coeur du politique." Grande and Keller-Rahbé, pp. 161–70.

Sanz, Amelia. "Villedieu, vous avez dit *classique*?" Grande and Keller-Rahbé, pp. 89–105.

Shewring, Margaret. *A Critical Edition of Sir Robert Howard's* The Great Favourite; Or, The Duke of Lerma. Garland, 1988.

Steggle, Matthew. *Digital Humanities and the Lost Drama of Early Modern England: Ten Case Studies*. Ashgate, 2015.

Sternberg-Greiner, Véronique. "*Si c'est ce qu'on appelle à présent des coquettes, / Il est vrai, je la suis*. Elvire et ses modèles dans *Le Favori* de Madame de Villedieu." Grande and Keller-Rahbé, pp. 185–97.

Teulade, Anne. "Le théâtre du doble: la réception de la *Comedia de privanza* entre tragédie et tragi-comédie." *Le théâtre espagnol du Siècle d'Or en France (XVIIe–XXe siècle). De la traduction au transfert culturel*, edited by Christophe Couderc, Presses Universitaires de Paris Ouest, 2012, pp. 101–15.

Tuilier, André. "La bibliothèque de Richelieu au Palais-Cardinal." Chancellerie, pp. 414–33.

Van Orden, Kate. "Du mérite de la danse pour le gouvernement des princes." Garden, pp. 135–47.

Vega, Lope de. *Rimas humanas y otros versos*. Edited by Antonio Carreño, Crítica, 1998.

Wollenberg, Jörg. *Richelieu: Staatsräson und Kircheninteresse: Zur Legitimation der Politik des Kardinalpremier*, Pfeffer, 1977.

4 Favorites in English drama

The first dramas featuring favorite ministers appeared in England during the last phase of Queen Elizabeth I's reign (1558–1603) when hopes of a royal marriage and the continuity of the Tudor dynasty were extinguished. Under these circumstances, anxiety about succession and the future government provoked state and public interest in the Queen's relationships with her closest ministers. Theater participated in this interest by commenting on the monarch's prerogatives to favor ministers. The topic of royal favoritism remained popular on the English stage under the Stuarts James I (1603–25) and Charles I (1625–49), whose reigns – especially James' – continued and even further developed the practice of sharing their sovereignty with favorite ministers.

This theatrical representation of favorite ministers coincides in time with one of the greatest epochs of drama production in England. Playwrights of the stature of Christopher Marlowe (1564–93), Ben Jonson (1572–1637), and John Fletcher (1579–1625) participated in the trend of writing plays about royal ministers. Some scholars, such as Bradner, Feros ("The Images of Evil"), DiGangi (*The Homoerotics*), and especially MacFaul, add William Shakespeare (1564–1616) to that list of remarkable dramatists. Nevertheless, *Henry VIII*, the only play by Shakespeare in which a royal favorite, the character Wolsey, had a major role, was co-written with Fletcher, who wrote broadly about favorite ministers (Worden, "Favourites" 171). In addition, Shakespeare's history plays generally omitted the representation of evil counselors (Worden, "A Frisson"), which were common in English dramas on favorites, and themes that were thoroughly explored and discussed in those dramas, such as sexual transgression and the nature of kingship, were barely interrogated by Shakespeare (Guy-Bray vii). In a period in which the revival of Tacitus in England led writers and dramatists to draw subtle and revolutionary parallels between past and present, Shakespeare concentrated on the epic conflicts of heroic figures, such as Caesar and Antony, featured by Livy and mainly Plutarch (Goy-Blanket 66–9).

Marlowe's *Edward II* (c. 1592) was one of the first and most influential plays on the subject of royal favoritism in England. It was printed in 1594 and reprinted three times during the following three decades. The play focuses on the tragic love story of King Edward II of England, whose intimate relationship with Piers Gaveston arouses the envy of other courtiers. A group of nobles led by Queen Isabella and her beloved Mortimer Junior successfully carries out an assassination plot against the monarch and his favorite.

Although set in the Middle Ages, this play points to the late phase of Queen Elizabeth I's reign. *Edward II* speaks overtly about sexuality, and more precisely about male homoeroticism, a regular theme in English theater on favorites. In particular, Marlowe's depiction of the homosexual relationship between Edward II and the French Gaveston could remind contemporary audiences of the supposed relationship between the Scottish King James VI and his French favorite and cousin, Esmé Stuart, VI Lord d'Aubigny (Rufo). James VI of Scotland was crowned James I of England in 1603, and in the ensuing years rumors about the king's sexual practices with his male favorites were habitual in the English court. A contemporary joke deriving from those rumors contrasted "King Elizabeth" with "Queen James" (Perry, *Literature* 134). In the early 1590s, when James, a cousin to Elizabeth, was already a candidate for the English throne, Marlowe seems to have known about James' plans to succeed Elizabeth and the playwright might have then had direct contact with the Scottish monarch and his advisors.[1]

Aside from King James' sexual life, Marlowe's work could have also been inspired by the likewise well-known homosexual relationships of King Henri III of France (1574–89) and his minions. "Minion," a cognate of the French *mignon*, was a derogatory term that Marlowe used often in his dramatic work, not only in *Edward II* but also in *The Massacre at Paris* (c. 1592), to refer to effeminate male favorites. Interestingly, the minions of Marlowe's plays were related to France and French culture. This association was understandable in the light of the contemporary context. Henri III of France was surrounded by male favorites – often nobles of lesser lineage – who were personally chosen by the king to the detriment of the traditional mechanisms of promotion of the most powerful nobility. This royal network of favorites or *système des mignons* gave rise to a literature that emphasized the homosexual connection between the monarch and his closest subordinates (Ferguson 147–90). The famed Pierre Ronsard, for instance, wrote in a satirical poem that Henri III's minions were "asses that have become cunts" (Rufo 21). In this vein, Pierre Matthieu published his play *La Guisiade* (1589), where he depicted the character d'Espernon (a clear reference to the Duke of Épernon, the most influential *mignon* of Henri III) as homosexual (Patterson 9). Matthieu also alluded to the controversial reign of Edward II and was most likely aware of the comparison that contemporary pamphlets made between Edward II-Henri III and Gaveston-Épernon. Marlowe, who knew both Matthieu's *La Guisiade* and Belyard's *Le Guysien* (Hillman), was also familiar with this sodomitical discourse about the favorites of the king (Rufo).

More importantly, this discourse had a great impact on Marlowe's contemporaries in England. For English aristocratic families, including those individuals destined to become part of the monarch's inner circle, spending time in France and acquiring a French education was common practice. This fascination with French culture, however, changed throughout the sixteenth century. Due to nationalistic impulses and political rivalries within the English court, the "Frenchification" or culture and manners noble Englishmen learned in the French court were seen as negative and associated with homosexual behavior. English courtiers with some relation to French politics were subject to rumors about their homosexuality and absence of national allegiance. From this perspective, those favorites who, regardless of their relation to France, occupied high positions on the pyramidal system of power and aroused the criticism of other courtiers were likely to be discredited as homosexual minions.[2]

Gossip about the homosexuality of some courtiers was widespread during the late sixteenth and early seventeenth centuries in England. Given that sodomy in early modern Europe was considered to be a crime and an act of treason (Betteridge), the accusation of disorderly homoerotic practices, particularly in France (Teasley) and England (DiGangi, *The Homoerotics* 1–28; Perry, "The Politics of Access"), was often used as a weapon against political rivals at court. This circumstance explains why in English theater, which generally depicted the figure of the court favorite in a negative way, audiences frequently were shown the deviational sexual conduct of the characters representing royal ministers. The discussion of royal favoritism in English theater was, to a great extent, introduced through the depiction of sexual relationships between the monarchs and their subordinates.

This propensity for explicitly bringing homosexuality to the stage was, however, unlikely to be seen in Spanish and French theaters during the seventeenth century. A playwright of that time in Spain or France would be unlikely to dare to make unambiguous reference to homosexual activities of a monarch with his favorite because, among other reasons, censorship laws were acted upon strictly and promptly.[3] Moreover, as Feros suggests, Spanish and French royal favorites of the early modern period, except during the reign of Henri III of France in the late sixteenth century, were never involved in sexual scandals concerning their relationship with the monarchs ("Historia y poesía" 138).[4] Some of those favorites, for example Lerma, Olivares, Richelieu, and Mazarin, were generally older than their rulers and developed to some extent a tutorial relationship with their sovereigns while the latter were still princes. In England, in contrast, Queen Elizabeth I and King James I were older than most of their favorite ministers – the Duke of Buckingham was almost thirty years younger than King James – and widespread rumors circulated that the favorites obtained their privileged position at court through their abilities to sexually please the monarch.[5]

Behind the recurrence of sexual behavior of monarchs with favorites in English drama, there was a major political denunciation of the muddling of what was conceived, in political theory of monarchy, as the king's two bodies: natural and political, or private and public. This phenomenon has been defined by Laurie Shannon, who, in the light of the contemporary English perception of French court politics, has used the French vocabulary and termed it *mignonnerie*. In theory, a monarch might form a friendly relationship (*amicitia*) with private persons who were different from the royal and official counselors. When that friendship became a factor in that private citizen's ability to gain access to a governmental office, the monarch's activity fell into *mignonnerie*, which is "the phenomenon at the juncture of friendship and (mis)rule." "*Mignonnerie* presents the political scandal of a monarch's unsuppressed private self, with the individuated and self-centered body natural eclipsing the body politic" (127) or "the monarch's subordination of public office to private love" (142).

The phenomenon of *mignonnerie* was common to royal favoritism in Spain, France, and England; yet it was only in England where the private friendship of the monarch with the favorite was frequently imagined to be a sexual – and homoerotic, in the case of King James – relationship. This characteristic, as observed in the representation of favorites in English drama, is not only due to the relative permissibility of censorship laws and to the erotic friendship between monarchs and favorites in England but also due to the bad reputation that royal favoritism generally had with the playgoers and to the greater denunciation of this political phenomenon, which in the Spanish and French theaters seems to have been less openly contested.

In Spain, numerous writings came to justify the position of royal favorite of the Duke of Lerma by means of his friendship relationship with King Philip III.[6] The dictionary of Francisco del Rosal, which was completed in the first years of the seventeenth century, defines "favorite" (*privado*) as "friend" (*amigo*) (qtd. in Redondo 56), and this definition is found in some of the earliest dramas on favorites in Spain. In Vélez de Guevara's *El espejo del mundo*, for instance, King Juan II of Castile calls Álvaro de Luna his "true friend" (3.2037), and King Alonso of Portugal appoints don Basco to the "office" of "grand friend" (*amigo mayor*) (1.890–1) to distinguish his personal favorite from the rest of courtiers who hold offices such as "steward" (*mayordomo*) (1.872), "grand master of the royal stable" (*mayor caballerizo*) (1.879), and "grand master of falconry" (*cazador mayor*) (1.882).[7] Furthermore, in Spanish drama the language of love is often used to describe that intimate friendship between the monarch and his royal favorite, as in the case of *Cómo ha de usarse del bien y ha de prevenirse el mal* (2.1550 and 1598) or Lope's *La inocente sangre*, which portrays a king loving his favorite "tenderly" (fol. 52v) and having with him a relationship that goes beyond kingship: "I was your King, and your friend" (fol. 58v). Despite these affectionate depictions, no Spanish drama seems to suggest a homosexual relationship between monarch and favorite,[8] not even Salucio del Poyo's *La próspera fortuna de don Ruy López de Ávalos*, in which King

Enrico and Ruy López, to whom the king calls "grand friend," are bedfellows (453). As Alan Bray studies, sharing a bed – a place for sleeping *and* talking – was a common expression of male friendship in the early modern period; similar to embracing and kissing, this was a "universally admired" display of friendship in sharp contrast to the "execrated and feared" sodomy (1).

Similarly, French *drames des favoris* present examples of *mignonnerie* in which a monarch singles out his chief minister based on the affection and friendly relationship between them; nonetheless, as is the case in Spanish theater, homosexuality is generally an absent subject in these plays.[9] This characteristic can certainly be seen in the dramas that Rotrou writes based on Spanish models.[10] In Desjardins' *Le Favori*, which seems to be modeled heavily on Spanish drama, the king of Barcelona expresses clearly his love for Moncade ("I confess, I loved just you," 1.341), and it is due to the favorite's coldness that he falls from grace (1.344). As some scholars have accurately noted, this love has no homosexual implication, for if it had, the play would have never been performed in Versailles, given Louis XIV's "violent distate" for homosexuality.[11] Rather, by portraying that intimate scene of royal favoritism, *Le Favori* celebrates in front of the French court the king's love toward his subjects (Steigerwald 172). French playwrights' disinterest in depicting effeminate royal favorites is clearly shown in Roman plays such as Corneille's *Othon* (1664), in which the dramatist borrows the features of his heroes from Tacitus' *Histories* though excluding from this classical source the details about their homosexual tendencies (Scherer 410). This deliberate omission can be also seen in the contrasting ways that Spanish, French, and English playwrights portray the life of Sejanus; while Spanish and French dramatists avoided exploring the homosexual practices of this favorite of Emperor Tiberius, English playwrights, for instance Ben Jonson, expanded on this topic.

Here is the importance of Christopher Marlowe's pioneering plays and the particular context in which they were written to the subsequent treatments of the favorite character in English drama. Most of the English plays featuring favorite ministers conceived royal favoritism in terms of *mignonnerie*, which, in turn, embraced again and again homoerotic relationships. Dramatists emphasized the private bonds that tied monarchs to their subordinates, and, as a consequence, in their plays they tended to examine and criticize the transgressive government of royal favorites. This transgression has a further-reaching impact on court life, beyond the political implications of *mignonnerie*. Royal favoritism also affects the socio-economic order at court. When a monarch alters the traditional mechanisms of promotion and social advancement and arbitrarily favors a courtier to the detriment of others, the social organization at court experiences profound changes. This redistribution of royal bounty ultimately leads to the monopoly of power and wealth by an all-powerful favorite, who becomes something of an *alter ego* to the king. Under these circumstances, the group of patrons and clients led by the king's favorite becomes the only effective network at court and displaces all other political factions. In sum, those who seek to prosper at court must somehow entangle themselves in the favorite's tentacles or web of influence. Francis Bacon, a contemporary and privileged witness of the ascendancy of the Duke of Buckingham, the greatest English favorite, observes this phenomenon when he writes to the Duke: "It is true that the whole Kingdom hath cast their eye upon you, as the new rising Star, and no man thinks his business can prosper at Court, unless he hath you for his good Angel, or at least that you be not a *Malus Genius* against him" (Spedding 15).

The Elizabethan court was facing these changes in the last years of its reign when Marlowe wrote his dramas on favorites. The play *Edward II* shows a clear identification of the favorite with the king's roles. The first time King Edward sees his dear Gaveston, he addresses him with these words: "knowest thou not who I am? / Thy friend, thy self, another Gaveston!" (1.141–2). The barons – the Mortimers and their followers – oppose and finally kill the two lovers in *Edward II*, that is, King Edward and his *mignon*, Gaveston, in doing so hoping to prevent the concentration of power within the King's favorite, as well as preserve the traditional social order, which, up to that point, had allowed them to both participate in the royal government and benefit from its bounty. These nobles, worried about the political dimensions of the king-favorite affair, made clear that the king's authority relied on them and that he could not share his crown so freely. Thus King Edward II laments: "My nobles rule; I bear the name of King. / I wear the crown, but am controlled by them" (20.28–9). In this regard, Marlowe's play evokes political ideas dominating the last years of the Elizabethan court. As Hammer showed in his study of this period, the election of favorites was more complicated than the queen's mere personal decision ("Absolute and Sovereign"). The monarch "was not always fully in control of her royal favour" (50), and her ability to choose favorites was constrained by the court as a whole and especially by its most powerful factions or pressure groups.

Although Gaveston stands out as the king's main minion in *Edward II*, he is not the only character that is featured as a favorite in this play. Once Gaveston is captured, Spencer Junior becomes the king's new confidant. However, the character whose features most resonate with those of a royal favorite is Mortimer Junior, Gaveston's antagonist. This young Mortimer fits into the category of the "overreacher" that Harry Levin, in his seminal work on Marlowe, defines as a typical Marlovian character whose greed and thirst for power are limitless.[12] Indeed, Mortimer's ambition does not end with the deposition of Gaveston; he also aims to dethrone King Edward II, which he achieves and thus becomes regent along with his partner Queen Isabella. At this point, Mortimer's hubris reaches its peak, and he challenges Fortune (23.67), which immediately precedes his tragic death at the hands of the young King Edward III in the last scene of the play.

The trajectory of Mortimer thus follows the *de casibus* or pyramidal structure of the rise and fall of powerful individuals that is deeply rooted in European literature and particularly in the representation of royal favorites.

The presence of more than one royal favorite in *Edward II* corresponds with the complex political tensions within the late Elizabethan court. In the first years of *mise en scène* of favorites, English playwrights depicted several favorite ministers in the same drama. At that time, in the early 1590s, the dramatic character of an omnipotent favorite was inconceivable. After all, Elizabeth I's Privy Chamber was comprised of Ladies who distributed favors but had restricted access to public offices (Wright), and the Queen never had a sole and all-powerful favorite. In addition, James I, whose Bedchamber became the locus of power, began to have single favorites only after 1612: first Robert Carr, Earl of Somerset, and then George Villiers, 1st Duke of Buckingham (Cuddy). Thus the process of centralization and concentration of power in the person of the male royal favorite accelerated through the end of Elizabeth I's life and reached its peak with the governance of the Duke of Buckingham, who managed to keep his position until his assassination in 1628, already years into Charles I's reign. After the execution of Buckingham, who was profoundly loved by Charles, this king refrained from having all-powerful ministers.

This political evolution ran in parallel with transformations in the dramatic representation of royal favoritism. After a decade or so of dramas featuring more than one favorite in the manner of *Edward II*, a milestone in that theatrical development was the performance of *Sejanus His Fall*, which is considered to be the first English drama concentrating on a single favorite. This play was written in the first years of the seventeenth century, an epoch of especially fecund imagination as it pertains to the dramatic representation of favorites, mainly due to the execution of the Earl of Essex (1601), who was a distinguished favorite of Elizabeth I. After this extraordinary boost, political favoritism continued to be a common theme on the English stage until the period of civil war in the 1640s. It should be noted, however, that during the Caroline era, the dramas on favorites became more and more focused on love conflicts, at the expense of much of their immediacy and political purport (Worden, "Favourites" 167–74).[13]

Sejanus His Fall

Sejanus His Fall[14] is a Roman tragedy centered on the figure of Sejanus, who was *praefectus praetorio* of Emperor Tiberius and, in the early modern period, became a paradigmatic image of the royal favorite. The importance of this play lies, among other things, in being the first of a series of dramas that, based on the reading of Tacitus and other ancient historians, featured royal favoritism in the early Roman Empire.[15] Despite its importance, this play presents numerous problems of interpretation that explain why the scholarship on this play is both extensive and controversial.

One of the first questions about *Sejanus* concerns its textual transmission. The text of the play that is known today corresponds to the printed versions that Ben Jonson published in 1605 in quarto and 1616 in folio. However, as Jonson reveals in the introductory note to the readers, the printed version "is not the same with that which was acted on the public stage, wherein a second pen had a good share" (215). To what extent the printed play was different from the text prepared for the performance and who the "second pen" was are questions that remain uncertain. It is commonly accepted that George Chapman (1559–1634) may have been the collaborator of the stage version, although it has also been suggested that Shakespeare, who was one of the cast members – possibly playing the role of Tiberius–, could have intervened in the composition of the drama (Barton 93–4).

A second source of controversy is the date of *Sejanus* and the place of its first performance. The records show that the play was entered in the Stationer's Register in November 1604 and a commendatory poem of the printed text indicates that it was performed at the Globe Theater. In addition, in the edition published in 1616 Jonson indicates that the play was first performed in 1603, which raises the question of whether this performance actually took place in the year of 1603 when public theaters remained closed for the most part or in the first three months of 1604, which still counted as 1603 according to the Julian theatrical calendar that was then used in northern Europe. The hypotheses, in the absence of evidence, suggest a court performance or an early performance at the Globe sometime during 1603 (Ayres 9–10; Cain, "Introduction" 199–200).

The concerns about when and where *Sejanus* was exactly acted for the first time are far from being trivial, since Elizabeth I died in March 1603 when James I's reign began, and it is still unclear the extent to which the play relates to either reign.[16] Further, *Sejanus* is contemporary to important events regarding the life and position of royal favorites, and scholars have repeatedly attempted to find analogies between Jonson's play and the favorites Earl of Essex, who died in 1601 though his legacy lived on in the ensuing years, Walter Ralegh, who was sensationally imprisoned in 1603, and Robert Cecil, who enjoyed a certain monopoly of power in the last years of Elizabeth's reign and remained in a privileged position in the early Jacobean period. Shedding light on these questions would help to clarify some apparent contradictions of Jonson's life during the first two or three years of the Jacobean period. Jonson repeatedly had problems with authorities during that time, including an official investigation of his *Sejanus*, while simultaneously he contributed with eulogies and entertainments to the ceremonies of coronation of James I. After those initial years of James' reign, which overlapped with the appearance and publication of *Sejanus*, Jonson left behind his troubles with the authorities and became a reputed poet and dramatist in the early Stuart court who received commissions and favors from kings and royal favorites alike (Evans, *Ben Jonson*; Marcus).[17] The relation of his Roman play to these changes in his position at court remains open to debate, although some scholars have strongly argued that *Sejanus* condemned the Elizabethan regime and conformed to James' initial aims to introduce changes in the distribution of power and patronage of the previous government. According to this interpretation, Jonson's drama, by showing the harmful effects of tyranny, functioned as a reflection of what James was, in theory, avoiding (Evans, "Sejanus" and Worden, "Ben Jonson and the Monarchy").

The questions about the purpose of *Sejanus* and the relations of patronage of its author are closely related to the problems of its sources. The execution of the Earl of Essex, in February 1601, was an aggravating indication of the autocratic course of Elizabeth's reign and probably the catalyst for writing *Sejanus*. The circle of Essex, which included prominent Tacitean writers such as Francis Bacon and Antonio Pérez, had been the main vehicle of transmission of Neostoicism in England throughout the 1590s.[18] The Earl of Essex himself, by means of his own writings and his encouragement and patronage to historians, promoted actively a historiographical movement, known as "politic history," with Tacitus as its model. The damaged relationship of Essex with the Queen in the last years of the sixteenth century contributed to the political radicalization of the Essexian faction, among which rebellious ideas against the government were shaped. For this faction, the tyrannical Rome of the principate that Tacitus described in his *Annals* was mirrored by the England of Elizabeth. These oppositional images intensified after the rebellion of Essex and his execution, which was followed by the punishment and repression of the Essex House and its adherents in the last years of the Elizabethan reign.

Ben Jonson was directly connected to the group around Essex through friends and patrons such as Henry Savile, a historian who translated and applied to his own work the historiographical principles of Tacitus, and Lucy Harington, Countess of Bedford, an influential literary patron who protected and promoted Jonson at court.[19] In turn, the dramas that Jonson wrote in the early seventeenth century are understood within the political culture against tyranny that emerged in the orbit of the Earl of Essex and the radicalization of that culture in the years around the earl's rebellion. In *Cynthia's Rebels* (1600) and *Poetaster* (1601) Jonson satirized Elizabeth's reign in relation to Essex's fall from grace,[20] although it was in *Sejanus*, in which Jonson extensively borrowed information from Roman histories and especially from Tacitus' *Annals* to depict negatively a corrupted court, where more clearly Jonson showed a frame of reference in common with the intellectual principles of the Essex group. The sources that Jonson used for writing *Sejanus*, which were detailed by the playwright himself in the numerous bibliographic citations in the quarto version of the play, were in accordance with the Neostoicism and the "politic history" of the Essex circle. However, Jonson's use of the works of those classical authors and how these sources shaped the political ideas of *Sejanus* are at the center of great disagreement among scholars.

According to Heinemann, the political and historiographical perspective that the Essex group developed through the rediscovery of Tacitus "had strong republican connotations" (136). However, the fact that Jonson cited and made copious use of Tacitus' work in *Sejanus* does not necessarily mean that Jonson adopted and shared the points of view of the Roman historian. In fact, it is even questionable whether Tacitus was himself an opponent of the monarchical form of government (Kapust). In this regard, the Neostoic Justus Lipsius conceived Tacitus as a proponent of monarchy, and in this spirit, he glossed his editions of the *Histories* and the *Annals* and wrote his *Politicorum* or *Six Books of Politics* (1589), an enormously popular political treatise in which Lipsius claimed that monarchy was the best form of government based on Tacitus. Jonson owned a copy of Lipsius' *Politics* filled with handwritten notes that have been exhaustively analyzed by Robert Evans, who concludes that Jonson's poetic and dramatic work, including *Sejanus*, reflects Lipsian political views (*Jonson* and "Sejanus").[21] Furthermore, Jonson acknowledged that he used Lipsius' elaborate Latin edition of Tacitus' *Annals* for writing his Roman play.[22] However, the aid of Lipsius to Jonson, as Daniel Boughner studied, was far more extensive. According to Boughner, Lipsius provided Jonson with much of the erudition, not only with the references to Tacitus, that appeared in the margins of the quarto of *Sejanus*. In other words, many of the marginal notes of *Sejanus* in which Jonson offered citations from Tacitus, Seneca, Suetonius, Dio Cassius, Pliny, and other classical authors were actually exact copies of Lipsius' glosses and footnotes to Tactitus' *Annals*.[23] On occasion, Jonson even attributed to Tacitus information that was only provided by Lipsius, thus distorting the work of the Roman historian. From this particular way of proceeding, however, one cannot infer that Jonson was unfamiliar with the classical sources that he claimed to have employed in the marginalia of *Sejanus*. In fact, there are other primary sources such as Juvenal and Claudian that he paraphrased in *Sejanus* and are absent from the marginal notes (Cain, "Introduction" 207). Moreover, one of the speeches in the play (3.407–60) was, as Jonson claimed elsewhere, his direct translation from Tacitus ("Informations" 481). In sum, the writing of *Sejanus* was based on Jonson's reading of classical sources, although the critical apparatus that he included in the margins was independent of the text in which the playwright evidently offered his own version of the historical events that he dramatized.[24]

Given Jonson's arbitrary selection of historical information as well as laxity and lack of rigor in citing his sources, one would feel tempted to agree with James Shapiro's assertion that the classical appearance of *Sejanus* was nothing but a mask that Jonson used to distinguish his work from other dramas on favorites, mainly Marlowe's *Edward II*, to which *Sejanus* was indebted (48–9). On the one hand, this theory has the advantage of distancing *Sejanus* from its classical roots, which have been the primary focus among scholars, and drawing attention to the similarities between *Sejanus* and earlier dramas on favorites. On the other hand, however, Shapiro's remark seems disproportionate and overlooks the cultural and political context in which Jonson wrote *Sejanus* as well as the relevance of Neostoicism, including the Lipsian Tacitism, to this play. Moreover, one must bear in mind that the public performance of *Sejanus* was a complete failure precisely due to its close adherence to historical sources and that it was not until the play was published soon after its removal from the public stage that it was held in high esteem; there, too, we see that its high regard comes from its "intellectual composition" or "scheme" (Chetwynd 43) rather than in its emotive and tragic elements. Although the dramatic quality of *Sejanus* and its ability to be performed have been largely discussed,[25] this debate finds, to some extent, a halfway point in what scholars traditionally call "closet" dramas and, more recently, Daniel Cadman has defined as "neo-Senecan" dramas. According to Cadman, *Sejanus* forms part of a group of English plays written in a neoclassical tradition and primarily intended to be read privately instead of staged publically. The key elements of these neo-Senecan dramas are stoicism, especially the ideas and works of Seneca and Tacitus, and republicanism, which is understood not as antimonarchism but as a means to control the power of the monarch with the aid of virtuous advisors.[26] The focus of these dramas, therefore, gravitates toward philosophical and political questions rather than actions and visual representation (Cadman 1–22).[27]

In what follows, I will first analyze the "native" roots of *Sejanus* and especially its relation with Marlowe's *Edward II*, and then I will discuss the importance of Neostoicism in Jonson's play. These two approaches, as I will argue, are compatible with each other, show the eclecticism of *Sejanus*, and reflect the development of Jonson's personal thoughts on royal favoritism.

The Marlovian Sejanus

The relation between the dramatic work of Jonson and Marlowe is clearly shown by the fact that Jonson attempted to write a drama on the favorite Mortimer that he later abandoned. Indeed, *Mortimer His Fall* is a tragedy that Jonson left incomplete as a rough draft manuscript, which was posthumously published in 1640. Although the surviving fragment of this play is interrupted in the second scene of the first act, it also includes the *dramatis personae* and the argument, which summarizes the contents of each of the five acts that the play would have had. Based on this information, *Mortimer His Fall* is classified as a traditional *de casibus* play featuring the rise and fall of Mortimer, who was also a central character in Marlowe's *Edward II*. In Marlowe's tragedy, as we have seen earlier, the character of Mortimer Junior was depicted according to some of the literary characteristics of a royal favorite. This Mortimer, toward the end of the drama, overthrew King Edward II and soon after he was himself deposed and executed by the young Edward III. Jonson's incomplete drama expands on this last part of the story of *Edward II*. It begins with the rise of Mortimer thanks to the favors that he receives from his lover Isabel, the Queen Mother, and ends with his execution and the celebration of King Edward III's justice.

Although there is no doubt that *Edward II* predates *Mortimer His Fall*, scholars still question whether Jonson started this unfinished project before or after he wrote *Sejanus*. Britland, in the introduction to the most recent edition of the text, is inclined to think, like Barton (338–9), that Jonson wrote *Mortimer* late in his career. However, authors such as Levin (100) and Worden ("Ben Jonson among the Historians" 76) assume that Jonson abandoned the writing of this play before beginning *Sejanus*, and former editors of the fragment play (Herford et al. 7:53) as well as Shapiro (45–6) defend this early dating of *Mortimer* based on internal evidence. This last hypothesis seems also more likely in view of the development of dramas on favorites in England. Indeed, the traditional dramatic structure of *Mortimer* around the rise and fall of a favorite who, in turn, plays a major political role in the play points toward the Elizabethan era, when the Renaissance *de casibus* motif had a strong presence as exemplified by the dramas of Marlowe and Shakespeare (Forker 25–6), rather than, as Barton and Britland suggest, toward the Caroline era, when the role of the favorite and his political participation were less central (Worden, "Favourites").[28]

In any case, and despite its shortness, the fragment of *Mortimer* contains numerous elements to be associated with Marlowe's *Edward II* and those elements constitute an essential part of the characterization of the Roman favorite in *Sejanus*. Shapiro briefly studies the relation between *Mortimer* and *Edward II* (45–8), although he focuses on the similarities between the characters Mortimer in both plays based on their historical analogy and not on their dramatic function. Thus Shapiro compares Mortimer's soliloquy in the last part of *Edward II* to the soliloquy of his homologous character in the first scene of Jonson's incomplete play. Nevertheless, one can also compare the royal favorite Mortimer, who is a central character if not the protagonist of Jonson's play, to the main minion of Marlowe's drama Piers Gaveston. *Edward II* begins with a soliloquy of Gaveston that resonates with the first lines of *Mortimer*. From his exile in France, Gaveston shows in that scene his enthusiasm for going back to England to be the favorite of King Edward II. This rise to the highest position of power makes him, as it usually happens to hubristic favorites, contemptuous of those below him:

> "My knee shall bow to none but to the King.
> As for the multitude, that are but sparks
> Raked up in members of their poverty,
> *Tanti!* I'll fan first on the wind
> That glanceth at my lips and flieth away" (1.19–23)

This pride and sense of superiority, which contrasts with the humble origins of Gaveston, is precisely what the protagonist of *Mortimer*, who confesses to having achieved the title of Earl through crimes (1.1.19–20), informs in his first words in the play: "This rise is made yet, and we now stand ranked / To view about us all that were above us!" (1.1.1–2), and in his "scorn of the nobility" that is mentioned in the argument (27).

This Mortimer shares another important feature with the Gascon Gaveston, namely his closeness to France and French culture. The short text of *Mortimer*, as Britland points out, contains numerous Anglicized French words, for instance "subtile" and "Engleterre," that are spoken by both Mortimer and Isabel (2). Jonson chooses this French spelling to distinguish this romantic couple and emphasize their corruption within the English court. In contrast to her troubled relation with the English nobility, the French Isabel only feels as though she were Queen of England when she is with Mortimer, as she tells him:

> "I ne'er was reconciled to these robes,
> This garb of England, till I saw thee in them.
> Thou mak'st them seem not boist'rous, nor rude,
> Like my rough, haughty lords *de Engleterre*,
> With whom I have so many years been troubled" (1.2.17–21)

Florence March analyzes briefly this fragment and concludes that Mortimer "helps tie the French queen to the English nation" (147), which suggests, given that the villainous Mortimer and the French Isabel engage in a politically pernicious relationship, an association between the royal favorite's evilness and the queen's foreign status. This association of Frenchness with corruption was likewise a key feature of *Edward II*, so much so that James Baker has recently read this "play as a xenophobic portrayal of a Frenchman [Gaveston] and as a shrewdly reactionary push against immigrants from Catholic nations" (ii). Jonson included French allusions and vocabulary in his plays repeatedly, especially in the first years of his career (March 154), which must be taken into account in the discussion of *Mortimer*'s date. In this regard, it is possible to think that the idea of depicting a corrupted favorite who could be related to French Catholicism was disregarded by Jonson after he converted to this creed in 1598, thus shifting the setting of his drama to the ancient pagan Rome.[29]

The romantic relationship between Queen Isabel and Mortimer in Jonson's play reminds us, of course, of the affair between those characters in *Edward II*, but it is also reminiscent of King Edward II's love for Gaveston. *Edward II* begins with the king asking his favorite, in a letter, to "share the kingdom with thy dearest friend" (1.2), thus making clear from the very beginning of the play that the monarch, by giving his private and "sweet friend" (1.160) exclusive access to the government administration, fails to rule properly and falls into *mignonnerie*. Likewise, in *Mortimer* Isabel raises her "sweet Mortimer" to the degree of earl and treats him as an equal (1.2.1–8). The erotic terms under which the queen approaches her favorite in the surviving fragment of the first act (1.2.10–6) are an indication that Mortimer enjoys "too much familiarity with the Queen," which the Chorus relates in the fourth act when, according to the argument of the incomplete play, King Edward III surprises the royal favorite in his mother's bedchamber. In both *Edward II* and *Mortimer*, the relationships of the monarchs with their favorites result in a social and political transgression, mainly because they "share the kingdom" with their private lovers, who are either low born or criminals. In turn, the same-sex relationship between Edward II and Gaveston is no less sodomitical than the heterosexual relationship between Isabel and Mortimer. Here sodomy is understood as a relationship involving a threat to the social order, and in this regard Isabel and Mortimer have been considered the most sodomitical characters of *Edward II* (DiGangi, *The Homoerotics* 112–5, Guy-Bray xvii-xviii), and, one may add, of *Mortimer* as well. The two main reasons to consider their relationship as sodomitical are the two lovers' conspiracy and murder of King Edward II, which is remembered with "horror" in the third act of *Mortimer* and precipitates the political downfall of the favorite, and the challenge to the patrilineal royal succession that Mortimer, with no title to rule England, represents.

The features that are similar to the favorites of *Edward II* and *Mortimer* are also found in *Sejanus*, which portrays a favorite that is Marlovian in many ways.[30] Mainly, Sejanus' rise to power, starting with his sexually corrupted childhood, and his position as the emperor's favorite are transgressive in every sense of the word. This transgression, which represents a severe threat to the political and social order, is seen in Sejanus' excessive pride, his venality as well as his serial crimes, and can be further illustrated by his sexual life. He is said to have been promoted to a higher social and political status after being a "serving boy," when "he prostituted his abusèd body" to a rich man called Apicius and thus he became a famous boy prostitute (1.212–6). This account of Sejanus' childhood is inspired by Tacitus' *Annals* (4.1) and Dio Cassius' *Roman History* (57.19.5), although neither Tacitus nor Dio describes Sejanus as "the noted pathic of the time," as Jonson does (1.216). From this one may deduce that in his play Jonson amplifies the implications of Sejanus' sexually corrupted childhood. Given the tendency of English dramatists to correlate political favoritism with same-sex intimacy, it is no surprise that Jonson wants to expand on this disorderly homosexual portrait of Tiberius' "minion" (3.243 and 4.366). Further, rather than homosexuality, Jonson means to emphasize the sexual transgression and immoderation that are associated with Sejanus' improper favoritism. From this perspective must also be recognized the heterosexual but equally disorderly extramarital affair that Sejanus has with a member of the imperial family, Livia, who is niece and daughter-in-law to Tiberius. These sexually deviated practices, furthermore, concern the favorite as much as the ruler. Sejanus is Tiberius' "stale catamite," and the Emperor holds in Capreae pedophiliac orgies with boys and girls who are treated as slaves (4.388–404).[31] This emphasis of *Sejanus* on sexual transgression also can be seen in the anonymous play *The Tragedy of Tiberius* (1607), which was written around the same time as *Sejanus* and is concerned with the same period of Roman history. In *The Tragedy of Tiberius*, Rome, upon Tiberius' ascension to emperor, turns into "a brothell house of sinne" (516) and both Tiberius and Sejanus engage in sexual relationships with the virgin girls of the Temple of Vesta, whose "Altars turnd to irreligious uses" (2710).[32]

Beyond all of the transgressions resulting from his ascension, one must underline the fact that Sejanus is an overreacher, which is a typically Marlovian feature and lends a good dose of tragedy to the character (Levin). As an overreacher, Sejanus' ambition is not satisfied by his exclusive position as the all-powerful minister of Tiberius, but he also aspires to displace the emperor and have full control of the government. This insatiable appetite for power leads him to seek marriage with Livia, which marks the beginning of his end as a favorite, since Tiberius then becomes fully aware of Sejanus' intentions and prepares his downfall. In order to achieve his goals of political ascendancy, the imperial favorite is willing to engage in a sexual relationship with Livia as well as with Lygdus, the eunuch who is, in turn, a "cup-bearer" of Livia's husband, Drusus Senior (2.12–24).[33] Therefore, sexual transgression is simply one of the instruments, such as crime or espionage, which Sejanus employs to succeed in his overreaching goals.

Jonson's depiction of Sejanus as an overreacher reminds us of the title character of *Mortimer*, who also aspires to hold the throne, and this last favorite is, in turn, related to the Marlovian overreachers of *Edward II*. The similarities among these characterizations suggest, as it has been argued, that Jonson's favorites are modeled on Marlowe's dramatic work. That is not to say, however, that *Edward II* was the primary source of those images of favorites. In fact, Marlowe's depiction of Gaveston resonates with the figure of the Earl of Leicester and, more particularly, with the image of this early favorite of Queen Elizabeth that emerges from the libel known as *Leicester's Commonwealth* (1584). This anonymous text, which gained immense popularity in the late sixteenth and early seventeenth centuries in England, portrayed Leicester as a corrupt favorite and compared him to historical figures such as Gaveston, the favorite minister of Edward II who Marlowe brought to the stage. Perry goes further and interprets a reference to Tiberius in *Leicester's Commonwealth* as an indirect allusion to Sejanus (*Literature* 233), concluding that *Leicester's Commonwealth* suggests a "continuum between Sejanus, Gaveston, and Leicester" and Marlowe's *Edward II* "evoque[s] a comparison between the staged Gaveston and the well-known image of Leicester as a Sejanus-like figure of corrupt favoritism" (*Literature* 192–3). Peter Lake also finds parallels between the careers of Leicester and Sejanus and draws attention to the familiarity of Jonson and his audience with the text *Leicester's Commonwealth* (142–4).

This common source indicates that both Marlowe's and Jonson's dramas on favorites shared a similar background and that the playwrights modeled their characters on images of corrupt favoritism that were widespread in the late Elizabethan court. However, the primary source of *Sejanus* was undoubtedly Tacitus, whose writings provided Jonson with historical material for dramatic representation as well as with a pragmatic view of politics and a sinister image of courtly life. If Marlowe and the author of *Leicester's Commonwealth* were familiar with the biography of Sejanus, the influence that Tacitus had on their works was of little or no consequence.[34] It was Jonson, according to Bradford, the Elizabethan playwright who unlocked Tacitus' *Annals* as a source for drama (135). In addition to Tacitus, *Sejanus* was highly influenced by the more general movement called Neostoicism, mainly through the oeuvre of Lipsius, whose impact on English culture was still barely noticeable when *Leicester's Commonwealth* and *Edward II* were written.

Based on these premises, it is plausible to establish some hypotheses about the origin of *Sejanus* in relation to *Mortimer* and *Edward II*. *Mortimer*, which in its form and contents bears numerous resemblances to *Edward II*, was probably conceived by Jonson sometime after 1594, the earliest date of publication of Marlowe's play and the year in which Jonson began his career as a playwright (Donaldson 99–122). At some point, Jonson decided to abandon his dramatic project on *Mortimer His Fall* to focus on the study and writing of *Sejanus His Fall*. Two events in 1598 could have contributed to that decision: his conversion to Catholicism and the appearance of Tacitus' *Annals* translated into English. Around that year, the Neostoic ideas and particularly the work of Tacitus began to disseminate widely in England, especially within the circle of the Earl of Essex to which Catholics like Jonson belonged. The rebellion and execution of this favorite minister in 1601 would have also been a determinant factor in the development and radicalization of Jonson's ideas on royal favoritism. While *Mortimer* and *Edward II* end celebrating the justice of Edward III who frees the court of corrupt favorites, *Sejanus* identifies royal favoritism as the consequence of a tyranny against which almost nothing can be done. This explains why *Sejanus* pessimistically begins and ends in similar circumstances, since the fall of Sejanus is followed by the ascendency of Macro, another evil favorite promoted by Tiberius. Despite its title, which probably derives from Jonson's attempt to stage Mortimer, the scope of *Sejanus His Fall* is not constrained to the fate of the Roman favorite,[35] rather the drama reflects on the exercise of tyranny as a whole and portrays a court society deeply entangled in the problems resulting from political favoritism. In sum, Jonson's characterization of Sejanus is Marlovian to a great extent, so much so that his original idea for a drama concerning favoritism, which was materialized in the incomplete *Mortimer*, was modeled on Marlowe's *Edward II*. However, at the same time, *Sejanus* contains ideas and concepts concerning political favoritism that Jonson adopted at the turn of the seventeenth century and that distance significantly this play from its predecessors.

The Neostoic Sejanus

In order to analyze the role of Neostoicism in *Sejanus*, a comparison between this play and *Le Favori* is in order. In this last French drama, Desjardins depicted a royal favorite within a group of courtiers, including Lindamire, who endorsed traditional values and was able to resist an antagonistic group of parasites that included Clotaire and Elvire, who represented a modern approach to court life based on an immoral opportunism and self-centeredness. In *Sejanus*, this unethical way of behaving has greatly advanced and completely conquered the highest political sphere, so that the favorite and his clients, including the majority of the Senate, are involved in evil and corrupted practices. The opposition to this faction comes from a group of characters known as the Germanicans, who owe their name to the deceased Germanicus, an early victim of Tiberius' regime. Neostoicism plays an important role in the Germanicans' defense of ancient values, although criticism on this subject is divided about the extent to which this opposition is effective or truly Neostoic and whether Jonson presents the Neostoic ideals in a favorable or negative way. In what follows we will discuss these issues and explore two hypotheses. One the one hand, it will be noted that Neostoicism in *Sejanus* is not confined exclusively to the Germanicans, but the Neostoic principles are spread throughout the play and are adopted, in different degrees, by various characters, including Sejanus. On the other hand, based on the Neostoic mixture of Senecan and Tacitean elements, it will be argued that what seems to be Jonson's ambivalence toward Neostoicism is actually a consequence of the playwright's Tacitism, which in *Sejanus* bears more weight than the Senecan tradition. In other words, while the Neostoicism of dramas on favorites such as *La paciencia en la fortuna* and *Le Favori* relies primarily on Seneca's philosophy, in *Sejanus* Tacitus' pragmatism is the leading influence, meaning the ethics of Stoicism are subordinated to the Tacitean realpolitik. Although these two hypotheses have been, to some extent, explored by diverse scholars,[36] my goal is to develop them further based on a close reading of *Sejanus* and the comparison of this dramatic text to those of *La paciencia* and *Le Favori*. In addition, I ultimately will interpret the tragic representation of favoritism in *Sejanus* as a mixture of Marlovian and Tacitean features.

If the immoral flatterers of *Le Favori* are stigmatized as chameleons, due to their fickleness and lack of principles, in *Sejanus* this role is played by both the favorite, who is identified with Vertumnus (3.136),[37] and his supporters, who "change every mood, / Habit, and garb, as often as he [Sejanus] varies" (1.34–5). Like Clotaire and Elvire in relation to Moncade, Sejanus' clients cease to be loyal to their patron as soon as he is condemned by the emperor, literally switching their seats in the Senate to distance themselves from the execrated favorite. This sudden change provokes the amusement of one of the Germanicans, Arruntius, who mocks at Haterius, a senator who cannot leave Sejanus because "His gout keeps him most miserably constant" (5.609). This joke is indicative of the contrast that Arruntius wants to make between the virtuous Germanicans and the inconstant circle of Sejanus, as one can see more clearly in that same scene when Arruntius compares the favorite's followers to dropping leaves that cannot resist a "little wind" (5.605). These words gain further significance when we think about the importance of nature within Neostoic philosophy and the fact that, in a previous scene of the same act, Sejanus bragged about his victory against the Germanicans in botanical terms:

> "I, that did help
> To fell the lofty cedar of the world,
> Germanicus; that, at one stroke, cut down
> Drusus, that upright elm; withered his vine;
> Laid Silius and Sabinus, two strong oaks,
> Flat on the earth; besides those other shrubs,
> Cordus and Sosia, Claudia Pulchra,
> Furnius and Gallus, which I have grubbed up;
> And since have set my axe so strong and deep
> Into the root of spreading Agrippine;
> Lopped off and scattered her proud branches, Nero,
> Drusus, and Caius too, although replanted" (5.241–52)

Marvin Vawter interpreted this garden metaphor as evidence of Sejanus' triumphs and the Germanicans' decadence (47–8). However, when seen in the light of Arruntius' later reply, once the favorite is doomed, Sejanus' metaphor is read as a sign of his own arrogance and tragic nature. From this point of view, it is the Germanican Arruntius who triumphs over the favorite and his clients, so much so that he even mocks at them. He may have good reasons to do so, not only because Arruntius and Lepidus are the two Germanicans who survive Sejanus' purge in Rome but also because they seem to have been instructed by the emperor. Indeed, Sejanus is condemned by means of a letter from Tiberius, who at that moment is away from Rome, that is read out before the Senate. In preparation for the condemnation of Sejanus, Macro, the new imperial confident responsible for bringing Tiberius' orders to Rome, distributed more letters among specific individuals, including Arruntius, Lepidus, Cotta, and Latiaris (5.161–2). These last two senators, who were allies with Sejanus, opened their letters on stage to learn that Tiberius required that they be present in the Senate and speak in favor of the emperor, "to strengthen his design" (5.272). Although nothing is said about Arruntius' and Lepidus' letters, we may assume that they were also instructions from Tiberius on how these Germanicans should act in the Senate. This means that Arruntius' participation in the sentence of Sejanus, perhaps including his jokes against the senators supporting the favorite, is intended to back Tiberius' "design." Once again, the dramatic role of Arruntius serves to accentuate the tragic character of Sejanus, since the favorite, against Tiberius' advice, had refused to take measures to subdue Arruntius, because, Sejanus told the emperor, Arruntius' tongue "will take away all thought / Of malice in your course against the rest" of Germanicans (3.499–500). These words become prophetic given that, at the end, Tiberius makes use of Arruntius to remove Sejanus from power and hide his complicity in the crimes against the Germanicans.

There is a general agreement among the critics of *Sejanus* that "Tiberius is the master-figure of the play" (Parfitt 39).[38] Based on his public speeches, one would think that Tiberius is an exemplary monarch. In his first appearance in the play, addressing the Senate, he distances himself from absolutism by drawing attention to his "human nature" in response to those "flatteries" that liken him to the gods (1.374–8). Instead of temples honoring his persona, Tiberius desires to be remembered, among other things, for his constancy (1.482). This image of an ethical ruler contrasts radically with the emperor that we see in the private sphere, in his conversations with Sejanus and Macro, in his plans to purge the Germanicans, or in the latter's continuous reports about Tiberius' evil thoughts and deeds such as murdering, torturing, and sexually abusing children of the Roman nobility in Capreae (4.373–401).[39] In this regard, the wicked royal favorite is merely a product of the tyranny of Tiberius who, nonetheless, manages to keep his minion in line. Thus Tiberius acts as a wise Renaissance prince by stopping Sejanus from becoming too powerful, since, as he says, "who nourisheth a lion must obey him" (3.660). The emperor both creates and eliminates his favorite when the latter becomes a threat to his sovereign position. To this end, he also succeeds in bringing together two opposing factions, the clients and the enemies of Sejanus, to endorse his own "design." In sum, Tiberius, whose morality is far from ideal, shows to be a master of the Machiavellian art of governing through his hypocrisy, pragmatism, and manipulative methods.

This Tacitean realpolitik, rather than the principles of Stoic philosophy, is the determinant factor in the outcome of *Sejanus*, as the examples of Sejanus' and the Germanicans' behaviors show as well. Unlike the royal favorites Gastón and Moncade, Sejanus is an evil favorite lacking Stoic virtues and moral servants and companions such as Pantoja and Manrique in *La paciencia* or Alvar and Lindamire in *Le Favori*. For instance, the "high prudence" of Livia (2.92), who aligns herself with Sejanus, has nothing to do with Stoic virtue but with her cunning decision to join the all-powerful minister. The unscrupulous Sejanus, who begins the play feeling insecure about the Germanicans ("I note 'em well," are his first words, 1.177) and impatient to realize his ambitious plans to become part of the imperial family ("Go to," 1.298; "Go," 1.351; "Go, and speed," 1.365), is later patient with Drusus Senior, who insults and strikes the favorite in the presence of the Germanicans. Drusus is Tiberius' son and heir to the throne; thus Sejanus bears "with patience" his insolence because the favorite says to himself translating from Seneca's *Medea*: "Revenge is lost, if I profess my hate" (1.577–9). Instead of giving vent to his anger and confronting Drusus, the apparently Senecan Sejanus proceeds coldly and successfully with his plans to poison Drusus, who is declared dead in the Senate at the beginning of the third act (3.54). This indicates that Sejanus does not pursue patience as a virtue itself; rather, for this immoral favorite, patience is no more than a means to achieve his ambitious political goals. This way of approaching patience is far from being simply Stoic or Senecan and differs greatly from that of Gastón de Moncada in *La paciencia* or Lindamire in *Le Favori*, plays that also include references to *Medea*. In *Sejanus*, virtues such as patience and constancy, which are fundamental in the Stoic philosophy of Seneca, have been infected with Tacitean realpolitik and reduced to a cynical view of court life as dominated by greedy people who pursue their own wealth.

This decisive influence of Tacitus in *Sejanus* can be also seen in the characters representing the Germanicans. To begin with, it is difficult to talk about the Germanicans as a homogeneous group (Bryant 201), and it is especially difficult to identify each of them as virtuous. The opinion that Jonson was "unable to create convincing virtuous characters" is particularly true in the case of *Sejanus*, in which virtue is presented through several characters.[40] Among the Germanicans there remains something of the moral basis on which the glorious Roman Republic and Empire were built, but the "fruits" or "seeds of the old virtue" disappeared with Germanicus (1.119–20). One of the most Stoic characters of the play, Silius, is unjustly accused of treason and commits suicide in the Senate. Although this final act may be in accordance with Stoic philosophy, it is certainly against the Christian principles of Neostoicism (Salmon 204). Moreover, this voluntary end has no consequence on the events of *Sejanus*; Silius does not become a martyr, and the passivity of the Germanicans remains unaltered (Vawter 45–6; Cadman 161).

Lucius Arruntius defines this suicide as "honourable" and a "great example" (3.340–3), although he refuses to emulate Silius. Before Silius stabs himself, Arruntius had advised him to believe the emperor without questioning, even though Silius was being unjustly accused (3.214–6). Arruntius also calls Tiberius a "monster" (4.373) in a private conversation with Lepidus, but in the Senate he follows personal instructions from the emperor. Because of his continuous comments and remarks, many of them as asides or in lines addressed to one character in the presence of more people, his contradictory and varying opinions, and his inaction against the tyranny of Tiberius, Arruntius is accurately described as a person who "only talks" (2.299). In this regard, the Stoic attitude that he inconsistently adopts throughout the play is only part of his discursive rhetoric rather than the guiding principle on which he bases his actions.[41]

A more Stoic and consistent character is Marcus Lepidus who, when asked by Arruntius what his arts to be safe are, answers:

> "None but the plain and passive fortitude
> To suffer and be silent; never stretch
> These arms against the torrent; live at home,
> With my own thoughts, and innocence about me,
> Not tempting the wolf's jaws: these are my arts." (4.294–8)

Lepidus, along with Arruntius, is one of the only two Germanicans who remain alive and free of oppression from the tandem Tiberius-Sejanus. However, the reasons for this success are not his Stoic virtues, which mean nothing to the emperor and his favorite. Lepidus is very aware of this circumstance when, in conversation with some Germanicans, he says that they live in times in which "virtue cannot safely be advanced, nor vice reproved" (3.482–3). If Lepidus survives and lives safely in this vicious Roman court, it is because of his silence and the fact that he offers no resistance to tyranny. In fact, and in spite of describing himself as innocent, living at home in Stoic retreat and away from the "wolf's jaws," Lepidus seems to be well integrated in the government administration and in harmony with its leaders. In the first act, when Sejanus is at the peak of his power, Tiberius gives Lepidus a grant for repairing and restoring monuments (1.511–3), and when Silius commits suicide, the emperor follows Lepidus' advice on how to divide the deceased's estate (3.359–65). Moreover, Lepidus' name is never mentioned in the conversations that Tiberius and Sejanus have about the Germanicans' opposition.

The Stoic virtues of the Germanicans are, therefore, mere appearance and worthless in the Tacitean court of Tiberius and Sejanus. Their criticism of tyranny and political favoritism achieves nothing and has no correlation with their actions, which are primarily intended to ensure their own safety. A conscious Arruntius thinks for a moment about warning the emperor and defying the flatterers and "palace-rats" who are spoiling the reign:

> "We that know the evil,
> Should hunt the palace-rats, or give them bane,
> Fright hence these worse than ravens, that devour
> The quick, where they but prey upon the dead.
> He [Tiberius] shall be told it." (1.426–30)

Yet Arruntius quickly abandons this idea because, as Sabinus, another Germanican, says: "It is not safe t'enforce a sovereign's ear" and "We must abide our opportunity, / And practice what is fit, and what is needful" (1.431–3). On grounds of this neglect, the play ends as distressingly as it began, because Macro replaces Sejanus as a similarly corrupt favorite, and Tiberius retains his position as the Machiavellian ruler of a tyranny against which the Germanicans, aside from lamenting privately and paying lip service to ancient values, have no opposition.[42]

In conclusion, the representation of royal favoritism in *Sejanus* is tragic in two main senses. First, it portrays the tragedy of a favorite based on the traditional *de casibus* structure of rise and fall that can be found in many dramas on favorites. Among these dramas, the characterization of Sejanus shares some important features with the *mise en scène* of favorites of Marlowe's *Edward II*. The title of Jonson's play, *Sejanus His Fall*, points toward those Marlovian features, which Jonson had already developed in the unfinished *Mortimer His Fall*. Nevertheless, Jonson was also influenced by the works of Tacitus, which provided him with new insights about political favoritism. This last influence might be noted in *Mortimer*, in which the royal favorite feels confident about his success despite his evil deeds, given that, he thinks, even "the wise man will ... safely do the ill" as a means to their ends, "as usurers rob or our physicians kill" (1.1.44–6). This cynical thought foreshadows the decadent milieu of *Sejanus* and also this play's second tragic dimension, which is that virtue, and particularly Stoic virtue, is nothing but a rhetorical discourse and hypocritical behavior subordinated to the primary concern for self-interest. The figure of Sejanus, who is corrupt and transgressive to the furthest extent, exemplifies this degradation of the Roman society, and especially of its opportunistic political elites who are unable to amend the tyranny of Tiberius.

Notes

1 Rufo 15, note 20. For a discussion of Marlowe's characterization of Edward II based on James Stuart, see Perry, "The Politics of Access" 1055–6, and the works that Rufo cites in footnote 14.

2 The words "homosexual" and "heterosexual" were coined in the nineteenth century, and from the time that Michel Foucault published his influential *History of Sexuality* (1976), where he argued that homosexuality was a relatively new historical invention, many scholars have been reluctant to use that terminology for the early modern context. Instead, critics generally prefer to refer to male same-sex desire during that period by means of synonymic terms such as "homoeroticism" and, especially, "sodomy," "which covered more hazily a whole range of sexual acts, of which sexual acts between people of the same sex were only a part" (Bray 3). However, Joseph Cady argues that during the Renaissance, homosexuality was a clearly defined category that was identified under expressions like "masculine love," and, in fact, scholars today, for example Jeffrey Rufo and Stephen Guy-Bray, conspicuously use the terminology of homosexuality in their studies on Marlowe's *Edward II*. Similarly, Michael Hawcroft studies the homosexual connotations that the terms *mignon* and *favori* had in seventeenth-century French drama (141).

3 "Whereas the emphasis in England seems to have been on sedition, in Spain the censors cast their net fairly widely, trawling for anything objectionable from slander or ridicule of private individuals, though coarseness and indecency, to irreverence and profanity" (McKendrick 185). Censorship in France, where there was no office of censor, was more repressive than preventive (Howarth, esp. 111–2). In addition, Ursula Heise explains how sodomy in Spain was

considered to be a graver sin than it was in England. While in England cases of sodomy "tend to be discharged with mere admonitions," in Spain, which presents "possibly the most violent history of persecution of homosexuals in Europe," sodomy carries the death penalty. Heise provides abundant data on these sentences against sodomites in Spain during the sixteenth and seventeenth centuries and concludes that there is a radical distinction between the English and "the Spanish attitude toward sodomy, and more specifically toward homosexual acts" (361–5).

4 Rumors, however, provoked an official investigation into whether Olivares administrated an aphrodisiac to the young Philip IV, thus implying a homosexual relationship between king and favorite (Weimer 266).

5 Both Elizabeth and James were accused of squandering royal funds to reward the "sexual prowess" of their favorites (Perry, *Literature* 131–2).

6 Feros, "Twin Souls" and *Duque de Lerma*, 201–33. Feros' useful analysis, however, places excessive importance on Pedro de Maldonado and his "revolutionary" manuscript pamphlet *Discurso del perfecto privado*, which Feros dates to 1609. Cf. Durand, who traces the biography of Maldonado, including his ephemeral and controversial relationship with Lerma, and suggests that the *Discurso*, written around 1603, is ambiguous about whether it supports or criticizes the favorite of Philip III.

7 Also in Salucio del Poyo's *La próspera fortuna de don Ruy López de Ávalos*, the king establishes a friendly relationship with his favorite: "Don't call me your Majesty. / Let's adhere to the rules of friendship, / call me your friend" (450).

8 As an exception to this generalization, see Weimer, who argues a homosexual relationship between the characters King Fadrique and his favorite don Juan de Cardona, who would represent the Count of Villamediana, in Tirso de Molina's *Privar contra su gusto*. However, the evidence found by Weimer in the text of Tirso to support his argument is both scarce and ambiguous. For instance, the identification of King Fadrique with both Philip IV of Spain and James I of England remains unclear. While Weimer's assertion that the relationship of the king with his favorite represents a "transgression," which can be called *mignonnerie*, seems accurate, it appears unlikely that Tirso conceives that relationship in homoerotic terms. This is still more improbable if we think that *Privar contra su gusto* portrays a positive and exemplary royal favorite and, as Weimer says, Tirso's intention behind this play is to support the Count of Villamediana and seek his patronage.

9 As exceptions, see the aforementioned *La Guisiade* (Patterson 9) and the analysis of *Clitandre* by Hawcroft, who consciously uses modern terminology to conclude "that the prince is homosexual and Clitandre bisexual" (140).

10 On Rotrou's plays, Amstutz asserts: "the friendship between the king and his favorite is exacerbated at the point when the favorite appears as his master's double" (406).

11 Gethner, in his edition of Desjardins' *The Favorite Minister*, p. 333, note 26.

12 See esp. Levin's interpretation of Mortimer as a Machiavellian character in relation to Fortune and the philosophy of Stoicism (98–104).

13 Cf. DiGangi, *Sexual Types* 192–220, who underlines the political intentions of English dramas on favorites during the Caroline era despite the fact that, as he acknowledges, "Charles ruled without a favorite" (219). However, DiGangi's discussion on Caroline drama seems too selective, since he chooses several plays on which to build his nevertheless compelling argument – that during those years "the favorite is depicted as a monstrous beast, [...] an easy target of hatred and paranoia" (194) – but excludes "plays in which favoritism is of peripheral importance; in which the favorite does not manipulate sexual alliances; in which the favorite is a farcical character; in which the favorite is

virtuous [...]; or in which favoritism is represented as an opposite-sex relationship" (255, n. 6). In addition, DiGangi's comment on Worden's study: "Beyond citing Massinger's *The Great Duke of Florence* and Ford's *The Broken Heart* as typical of a dramatic trend [...], Worden has little to say about the many Caroline representations of favoritism" (254, n. 3), does not do justice to a broad survey that covers more than a century of English drama and is, as Worden says, "primarily concerned to identify the general tendency of theatrical treatments of favouritism, not the plentiful variations or contrasts to be found among them" ("Favourites" 160). Furthermore, Worden actually includes in his analysis multiple "Caroline representations of favoritism" other than *The Great Duke of Florence* and *The Broken Heart*, such as *The Deserving Favourite, The Fool Would Be a Favourite, The Floating Island, The Court Beggar*, and *The Fair Favourite*, thus showing a perhaps more diverse representation of favorites during the reign of Charles I than DiGangi, who discusses no more than seven Caroline plays, does. In addition, the method that DiGangi uses to highlight the importance of dramas concerning favorites in the Caroline era, based on the account of printed plays in which the *Index of Characters in Early Modern English Drama* (Berger et al.) identifies "favourite(s)," is far from exhaustive or even reliable, since DiGangi asserts (254–5, n. 5), with good reasons, that the *Index of Characters* provides an incomplete list of dramas concerning favorites, but he unfortunately mentions the absence of *The Deserving Favourite*, when in reality this play can be found in the *Index of Characters* (123, no. 423). Finally, DiGangi also ignores that the *Index of Characters* includes, although without identifying "Favourite(s)" in them, indisputable dramas featuring favorites such as Jonson's *Sejanus His Fall* (1603) (114, no. 216), which is analyzed as such by DiGangi himself in a previous and insightful book: *The Homoerotics.*

14 Unless otherwise stated, all quotations and references to this play, henceforth referred to as *Sejanus*, will be to Tom Cain's edition.

15 In addition to Ben Jonson, three anonymous authors wrote *The Tragedy of Tiberius* (1607), which staged Sejanus as well, *The Tragedy of Nero* (1624), and *The Emperor's Favourite* (c. 1629), these last two plays set during the reign of Nero; moreover, Massinger's *The Roman Actor* (1626) and May's *Julia Agrippina* (1628) featured the reigns of Domitian and Claudius, respectively. The Spanish and French playwrights (Juan Pérez de Montalbán, Jean Magnon, and Cyrano de Bergerac) who dramatized the life of Sejanus were apparently unaware of Jonson's play.

16 For a good discussion on this problem, see Worden, "Ben Jonson and the Monarchy."

17 One of Jonson's most important patrons during the reign of James was Esmé Stuart, VII Lord d'Aubigny and minion of James in the king's bedchamber, and to whom the folio version (1616) of *Sejanus* was dedicated.

18 On the dissemination of Neostoicism, mainly Seneca and Tacitus, in England through the Essexian faction, I follow the documented articles by Bradford and Salmon.

19 On the connection of Jonson and his dramatic work with the circle of Essex, see Cain, "Satyres," and in particular, on Jonson and the Countess of Bedford, see Taylor 168–208. For the relationship of Jonson with other historians in the orbit of Essex and how the work of playwrights and historians blended together under the influence of Tacitus, see Bradford 133–5 and Worden, "Ben Jonson among the Historians."

20 See Cain, "Satyres," who also mentions other plays alluding to Essex by Jonson's contemporaries.

21 On Jonson's own variation of the Lipsian paradigm, see also McCrea 138–70.

22 Besides Lipsius' edition, Jonson also made considerable use of Richard Greneway's English translation of the *Annals* (1598), despite the playwright's criticism of the quality of the translation (Ayres 14–6; Cain, "Introduction" 207).

23 A similar deceptive method is seen in Jonson's use of *De formulis* by Brisson, "from whom many references to classical sources are taken and cited as if directly from the original" (Cain, "Introduction" 207). Lipsius and Brisson, in any case, were not the only authorities on classical sources that Jonson employed (Herford et al. 1.252).

24 The fact that Jonson excluded the marginalia for the folio edition of *Sejanus* indicates that those erudite notes were dispensable.

25 See, for instance, arguments for and against the value of *Sejanus* as a tragedy in Marotti, Barton 92–105, and Ayres 22–8.

26 On this form of republicanism in the dramatic corpus of Jonson, see Sanders, esp. 1–33, and Perry, *Literature* 229–48, who analyzes *Sejanus* within a "republican theory of favoritism" that is further developed in later Roman plays.

27 Prior to Cadman, other scholars pointed toward similar conclusions. Robert Knoll, for example, highlighted that *Sejanus*, a Senecan drama whose "plot is an excuse for a moral essay," "ought to be judged by standards different from those applied to many contemporaneous tragedies" (70).

28 For the contrast between Elizabethan and Caroline theatrical representation of favorites, see also DiGangi, *Sexual Types* 192–220.

29 For a reading on *Sejanus* as a Catholic play, see Pickett (26–30), who associates Sejanus' dismissal of pagan practices with the Protestant outlook of Catholic rituals, and especially Lake, who identifies the group of characters known as the Germanicans, who oppose the Roman favorite, with the marginalized Catholics who lived in the Protestant Elizabethan reign. Perry considers it plausible that *Sejanus* "as originally conceived may have reflected a fusion of Catholic libel with the politics of Tacitean complaint developed in the Essex circle" (*Literature* 247). The fact that many Catholics found protection in the circle of Essex, including Thomas Wright, who enjoyed the earl's patronage and is thought to have converted Jonson (Lake 154), reinforces Perry's observation.

30 James Shapiro identifies some Marlovian aspects in Jonson's representation of Sejanus based on Marlowe's complete dramatic corpus (48–51). In this way he equates, for example, the tragic end of the Roman favorite with the dismemberment of the protagonist of Marlowe's *Doctor Faustus*. To this one may add that the horrendous death of Edward II, whose anus is penetrated with a hot poker in a "dungeon" (*Edward II* 24.37), could have also inspired Jonson's account of the death of Sejanus, who is first taken to a "dungeon" because "he deserves it" (5.671). DiGangi suggests that there is a correlation between the low, underground location of a dungeon and the lower part of Edward II's body that is attacked (*The Homoerotics* 113–4). On Edward II's death as a "violent parody of anal intercourse," see Rufo 22. Perhaps Sejanus, who began his career as a prostitute boy, was thought to deserve a similar sodomitical torture.

31 DiGangi (*The Homoerotics* 122–4) doubts whether "catamite" refers to Sejanus or Tiberius, although scholars (e.g. MacFaul 54, Perry, *Literature* 240–1, and Cain in his edition of *Sejanus*) generally believe that the favorite is characterized as a catamite to the emperor.

32 In contrast to these perverted depictions of Sejanus' term as Tiberius' favorite and of Rome as Sodom, which for the most part are in accordance with the accounts of the classical sources, the Spanish and French playwrights who dramatized the life of Sejanus did not expand on his sexual practices. *Amor, privanza y castigo* (c. 1621), by Juan Pérez de Montalbán, is one of the few Spanish *comedias* portraying an evil favorite. According to Cauvin, this is the

only Spanish drama on favorites "to depict a protagonist as the epitome of villainy from beginning to end" (402). However, the relationship between this evil inclination of Sejanus and his sexual practices is not explored by Montalbán, but only vaguely suggested by means of his affair with Livia. Likewise, Savinien Cyrano de Bergerac, in *La mort d'Agrippine* (1653), "des-érotise la figure de Séjan" (Darmon xiii). Moreover, both in *La mort d'Agrippine* and in Jean Magnon's *Sejanus* (1647) Tiberius' favorite is portrayed positively (Amstutz 381–93).

33 As Tom Cain's critical apparatus of this passage notes, Jonson implies a homosexual relationship between Drusus and his eunuch Lygdus, "derived from Jove's relationship with his cup-bearer Ganymede." In turn, once Sejanus learns that Lygdus is "young," "fair," and "a delicate youth," he commands: "Send him to me, I'll work him" (2.23–4). Given the context in which these words are spoken, the homoerotic trajectory of both Sejanus and Lygdus, and the fact that Jonson quotes Tacitus in the footnote (Sejanus "ensnared the eunuch in a debauched relationship," *Ann.* 4.10), it is plausible to read Sejanus' intentions to "work" Lygdus in sodomitical terms.

34 Suetonius, who, unlike Tacitus, is cited in *Leicester's Commonwealth*, was probably the source of information on Roman history of the early empire used by the author of this text.

35 Cf. Knoll, who reads *Sejanus* as a *de casibus* play in the tradition of English tragedy and claims that the play's subject "is not the man who was Tiberius' favorite, but the arrogance which doomed him" (71).

36 Numerous scholars (for instance, Bryant, Knoll, Parfitt, Vawter, Maus 22–46, Barton 99–103, Burgess, Perry, *Literature* 229–48, Chetwynd) have analyzed the role of Neostoicism among the Germanicans, reaching different conclusions; however, the representation of virtue in other characters of *Sejanus* has been scarcely studied. Likewise, the decisive influence of Tacitus in *Sejanus* has been diversely emphasized; see, for example, Bradford, esp. 134–5, Maus 36–9, and Worden, "Ben Jonson among the Historians."

37 "Etruscan god who became associated with all forms of changing and turning (Lat. *verto, –ere*), especially the turning of the seasons" (*Sejanus* 3.136, footnote by Tom Cain). Further, the character Sejanus in *The Tragedy of Tiberius* expresses admiration for the chameleonic and inconstant courtier:

> "He that wil clime, and aime at honours white,
> Must be a wheeling turning pollititian:
> A changing Proteus, and a seeming all,
> Yet a discoloured Camelion
> Fram'd of an ayrie composition:
> As fickle and vnconstant as the ayre" (667–72)

38 Among the critics who give prominence to the character of Tiberius, see, for instance, Barton, who regards him as "the most appalling, but also the most riveting character in the tragedy" (104). Knoll believes that "Tiberius is God's agent on earth" and "the instrument of stability" (78), while DiGangi highlights Tiberius' proficiency in using sodomitical sexuality as a source of power to retain his position and pleasure (*The Homoerotics* 121–4). Of utmost interest is the reading of Tiberius' art of government as Jonson's art of writing (Marotti, esp. 211–9; Archer 107–12), especially in the last part of *Sejanus*, when the absent emperor acts as the playwright by arranging the staging of Sejanus' trial in the Senate, which is compared to a theater in which the senators-players read out Tiberius' letters and act according to his script.

39 Arruntius, for instance, notices that Tiberius acts distinctly in public and in private by having Sejanus, his "private parasite redeem" what the emperor "in public subtlety will lose / to making him a name" (1.386–8).
40 Parfitt, esp. 23 and 29. See also Maus, who studies the evolution of the Stoic character, which tends to gradually disappear, in Jonson's plays (22–46).
41 For an analysis of the power of rhetoric in *Sejanus*, see Marotti 198–207. The Stoicism and the role as a commentator of Arruntius have been recently discussed by Geng.
42 Several authors compare the Germanicans and their way to express their sentiments to a chorus (see, for instance, Bryant 198–9, Nash 170, and Marotti). Cf. Vawter, who, rather than relegating them "to a position of honest choric commentators," believes that the Germanicans "exemplify in fact what the sickness of the social order is – indeed, what the source of evil is in the world of the play as Jonson saw it" (42). Following this interpretation, Chetwynd also analyzes "the shared complacency of Sejanus and Arruntius" (50–5).

Works Cited

Amstutz, Delphine. *La Fable du favori dans la littérature française du premier XVIIe siècle*. Dissertation, Université Paris-Sorbonne, 2013.

Archer, John. *Sovereignty and Intelligence: Spying and Court Culture in the English Renaissance*. Stanford UP, 1993.

Ayres, Philip. "Introduction." *Sejanus His Fall*, by Ben Jonson, Manchester UP, 1990, pp. 1–44.

Baker, James. *Staging Sex or Fighting Foreignness? Marlowe's Edward II as Xenophobic Drama*. Master's Thesis, U of Southern Mississippi, 2015.

Barton, Anne. *Ben Jonson, Dramatist*. Cambridge UP, 1984.

Berger, Thomas et al. *An Index of Characters in Early Modern English Drama: Printed Plays, 1500–1660*. Rev. ed. Cambridge UP, 1998.

Betteridge, Tom, editor. *Sodomy in Early Modern Europe*. Manchester UP, 2002.

Bevington, David, et al., editors. *The Cambridge Edition of the Works of Ben Jonson*. 7 vols., Cambridge UP, 2012.

Boughner, Daniel. "Jonson's Use of Lipsius in *Sejanus*." *Modern Language Notes*, vol. 73, 1958, pp. 247–55.

Bradford, Alan. "Stuart Absolutism and the 'Utility' of Tacitus." *Huntington Library Quarterly*, vol. 46, no. 2, 1983, pp. 127–55.

Bradner, Leicester. "The Theme of *privanza* in Spanish and English Drama 1590–1625." *Homenaje a William L. Fichter. Estudios sobre teatro antiguo hispánico y otros ensayos*, edited by A. David Kossoff and José Amor, Castalia, 1971, pp. 97–106.

Bray, Alan. "Homosexuality and the Signs of Male Friendship in Elizabethan England." *History Workshop Journal*, vol. 29, no. 1, 1990, pp. 1–19.

Britland, Karen. "Mortimer His Fall: Textual Essay." Bevington et al., electronic edition, pp. 1–3.

Bryant, Joseph. "The Nature of the Conflict in Jonson's *Sejanus*." *Vanderbilt Studies in the Humanities*, vol. 1, edited by Richmond Beatty et al., Valderbilt UP, 1951, pp. 197–219.

Burgess, Glenn. "The 'Historical Turn' and the Political Culture of Early Modern England: Towards a Postmodern History?." Wells et al., pp. 31–47.

Cadman, Daniel. *Sovereigns and Subjects in Early Modern Neo-Senecan Drama: Republicanism, Stoicism and Authority.* Ashgate, 2015.

Cady, Joseph. "'Masculine Love,' Renaissance Writing, and the 'New Invention' of Homosexuality." *Journal of Homosexuality*, vol. 23, no. 1–2, 1992, pp. 9–40.

Cain, Tom. "Introduction." Jonson, *Sejanus His Fall*, pp. 197–209.

———. "'Satyres, That Girde and Fart at the Time': *Poetaster* and the Essex Rebellion." Sanders et al., pp. 48–70.

Cassius, Dio. *Roman History.* 9 vols. Edited by Earnest Cary and Herbert Foster, Harvard UP, 2014.

Cauvin, Mary Austin. *The* comedia de privanza *in the Seventeenth Century.* Dissertation, U of Pennsylvania, 1957.

Chetwynd, Ali. "'He that Lends You Pity Is Not Wise': Rereading *Sejanus* for Pity and Terror." *The Ben Jonson Journal*, vol. 14, no. 1, pp. 43–60.

Cómo ha de usarse del bien y ha de prevenirse el mal. Edited by Paola Laskaris, Mauro Baroni, 2008.

Cuddy, Neil. "The Revival of the Entourage: The Bedchamber of James 1, 1603–1625." Starkey, pp. 173–225.

Darmon, Jean-Charles. "L'athée, la politique et la mort: variations sur 'de belles impiétés.'" *La mort d'Agrippine*, by Cyrano de Bergerac, Encre marine, 2005, pp. i–lxiii.

Desjardins, Marie-Catherine (Madame de Villedieu). *Le Favori.* Edited by Delphine Amstutz, Hermann, 2017.

———. *The Favorite Minister. The lunatic lover and other plays by French women of the 17th and 18th centuries*, edited by Perry Gethner, Heinemann, 1994, pp. 39–88.

DiGangi, Mario. *Sexual Types: Embodiment, Agency, and Dramatic Character from Shakespeare to Shirley.* U of Pennsylvania P, 2011.

———. *The Homoerotics of Early Modern Drama.* Cambridge UP, 1997.

Donaldson, Ian. *Ben Jonson: A Life.* Oxford UP, 2011.

Durand, José. "Andanzas del padre Maldonado y su *Privado* ejemplar." *Nueva Revista de Filología Hispánica*, vol. 29, no. 2, 1980, pp. 312–42.

Elliott, John, and Laurence Brockliss, editors. *The World of the Favourite.* Yale UP, 1999.

Evans, Robert. *Ben Jonson and the Poetics of Patronage.* Bucknell UP, 1989.

———. *Jonson, Lipsius and the Politics of Renaissance Stoicism.* Longwood, 1992.

———. "*Sejanus*: Ethics and Politics in the Early Reign of James." Sanders et al., pp. 71–92.

Ferguson, Gary. *Queer (Re)Readings in the French Renaissance: Homosexuality, Gender, Culture.* Ashgate, 2008.

Feros, Antonio. *El Duque de Lerma: Realeza y privanza en la España de Felipe III.* Marcial Pons, 2002.

———. "Historia y poesía: monarcas y favoritos en las obras de Marlowe y Mira de Amescua." *Del poder y sus críticos en el mundo ibérico del Siglo de Oro*, edited by I. Arellano et al., Iberoamericana-Vervuert, 2013, pp. 111–42.

———. "Images of Evil, Images of Kings: The Contrasting Faces of the Royal Favourite and the Prime Minister in Early Modern European Political Literature, *c.* 1570–*c.* 1650," Elliott and Brockliss, pp. 205–22.

———. "Twin Souls: Monarchs and Favourites in Early Seventeenth-Century Spain." *Spain, Europe, and the Atlantic World: Essays in Honour of John H. Elliott*, edited by R. Kagan and G. Parker, Cambridge UP, 1995, pp. 27–47.

Forker, Charles. "Introduction." *Edward the Second*, by C. Marlowe, Manchester UP, 1994.

Geng, Penelope. "'He Only Talks': Arruntius and the Formation of Interpretative Communities in Ben Jonson's *Sejanus*." *The Ben Jonson Journal*, vol. 18, no. 1, 2011, pp. 126–40.

Goy-Blanquet, Dominique. "Elizabethan Historiography and Shakespeare's Sources." *The Cambridge Companion to Shakespeare's History Plays*, edited by M. Hattaway, Cambridge UP, 2002, pp. 57–70.

Guy-Bray, Stephen. "Introduction." Marlowe, *Edward II*, pp. vii–xxiv.

Hammer, Paul. "'Absolute and Sovereign Mistress of her Grace'? Queen Elizabeth I and her Favourites, 1581–1592." Elliott and Brockliss, pp. 38–53.

Hawcroft, Michael. "Homosexual Love in Corneille's *Clitandre* (1632)." *Seventeenth-Century French Studies*, vol. 15, no. 1, 1993, pp. 135–44.

Heinemann, Margot. "Rebel Lords, Popular Playwrights, and Political Culture: Notes on the Jacobean Patronage of the Earl of Southampton." *Patronage, Politics, and Literary Traditions in England, 1558–1658*, edited by C. Brown, Wayne State UP, 1993, pp. 135–58.

Heise, Ursula. "Transvestism and the Stage Controversy in Spain and England, 1580–1680." *Theatre Journal*, vol. 44, no. 3, 1992, pp. 357–74.

Herford, Charles, et al., editors. *Ben Jonson*. 11 vols, The Clarendon P, 1925–52.

Hillman, Richard. "Marlowe's Guise: Offending against God and King." *Notes and Queries*, vol. 55, no. 2, 2008, pp. 154–9.

Howarth, William D. *French Theatre in the Neo-classical Era, 1550–1789*. Cambridge UP, 1997.

Jonson, Ben. "Informations to William Drummond of Hawthornden." Edited by Ian Donaldson. Bevington et al., vol. 5, pp. 351–98.

———. *Mortimer His Fall*. Edited by Karen Britland. Bevington et al., vol. 7, pp. 403–16.

———. *Sejanus His Fall*. Edited by Tom Cain. Bevington et al., vol. 2, pp. 195–391.

Kapust, Daniel. "Tacitus and Political Thought." *A Companion to Tacitus*, edited by Victoria Pagán, Blackwell, 2012, pp. 504–28.

Knoll, Robert. *Ben Jonson's Plays: An Introduction*. U of Nebraska P, 1964.

La paciencia en la fortuna. CC*IV 28033, *Comedias de Diferentes Autores*, vol. 74, no. 2. Biblioteca Palatina di Parma, Parma. 1–55r.

Lake, Peter. "From *Leicester his Commonwealth* to *Sejanus His Fall*: Ben Jonson and the Politics of Roman (Catholic) Virtue." *Catholics and the "protestant Nation": Religious Politics and Identity in Early Modern England*, edited by E. Shagan, Manchester UP, 2005, pp. 128–61.

Leicester's Commonwealth. 1584. Edited by Dwight Peck, Ohio UP, 1985.

Levin, Harry. *The Overreacher: A Study of Christopher Marlowe*. Harvard UP, 1952.

MacFaul, Tom. "'A Kingdom with my Friend': Favorites in Shakespeare." *Literary Milieux: Essays in Text and Context Presented to Howard Erskine-Hill*. Edited by D. Womersley and R. McCabe, U of Delaware P, 2008, pp. 52–71.

March, Florence. "'O Confusion of Languages, and Yet No Tower of Babel!': French Allusions and Ben Jonson's Linguistic Project." *Representing France and the French in Early Modern English Drama*, edited by Jean-Christophe Mayer, U of Delaware P, 2008, pp. 142–57.

Marcus, Leah S. "Jonson and the Court." *The Cambridge Companion to Ben Jonson*, edited by Richard Harp and Stanley Stewart, Cambridge UP, 2000, pp. 30–42.

Marlowe, Christopher. *Edward II*. Rev. edition by Martin Wiggins and Robert Lindsey, Bloomsbury, 2014.

Marotti, Arthur. "The Self-Reflexive Art of Ben Jonson's *Sejanus*." *Texas Studies in Literature and Language*, vol. 12, no. 2, 1970, pp. 197–220.

Maus, Katharine. *Ben Jonson and the Roman Frame of Mind*. Princeton UP, 1984.

McCrea, Adriana. *Constant Minds: Political Virtue and the Lipsian Paradigm in England, 1584–1650*. U of Toronto P, 1997.

McKendrick, Melveena. *Playing the King: Lope de Vega and the Limits of Conformity*. Woodbridge, Tamesis, 2000.

Nash, Ralph. "Ben Jonson's Tragic Poems." *Studies in Philology*, vol. 55, no. 2, 1958, pp. 164–186.

Parfitt, George. "Virtue and Pessimism in Three Plays by Ben Jonson." *Studies in the Literary Imagination*, vol. 6, no. 1, 1973, pp. 23–40.

Patterson, Jonathan. "'Diables incarnez, Machiavelistes, heretiques': The Villains of Pierre Matthieu's *La Guisiade* Reconsidered." *French Studies: A Quarterly Review*, vol. 70, no. 1, 2016, pp. 1–16.

Pérez de Montalbán, Juan. *Amor, privanza y castigo. Primero tomo de las Comedias del Doctor Juan Pérez de Montalbán*. A. Vázquez, 1638.

Perry, Curtis. *Literature and Favoritism in Early Modern England*. Cambridge UP, 2006.

———. "The Politics of Access and Representations of the Sodomite King in Early Modern England." *Renaissance Quarterly*, vol. 53, no. 4, 2000, pp. 1054–83.

Pickett, Holly. "The Idolatrous Nose: Incense on the Early Modern Stage." *Religion and Drama in Early Modern England: The Performance of Religion on the Renaissance Stage*, edited by J. Degenhardt and E. Williamson, Ashgate, 2011, pp. 19–37.

Redondo, Agustin. "'Un bon favori est un favori mort.' Le duc de Lerma, Rodrigo Calderón et le problème du favor face à l'opinion publique." *La représentation du favori dans l'Espagne de Philippe III et de Philippe IV*, edited by H. Tropé, Presses Sorbonne nouvelle, 2010, pp. 53–74.

Rufo, Jeffrey. "Marlowe's Minions: Sodomitical Politics in *Edward II* and *The Massacre at Paris*." *Marlowe Studies: An Annual*, vol. 1, 2011, pp. 5–23.

Salmon, J. H. M. "Stoicism and Roman Example: Seneca and Tacitus in Jacobean England." *Journal of the History of Ideas*, vol. 50, no. 2, 1989, pp. 199–225.

Salucio del Poyo, Damián. *La próspera fortuna de don Ruy López de Ávalos. Dramáticos contemporáneos de Lope de Vega*, vol. 43.1, edited by R. de Mesonero Romanos, M. Rivadeneyra, 1857, pp. 437–63.

Sanders, Julie. *Ben Jonson's Theatrical Republics*. MacMillan, 1998.

Sanders, Julie, et al. *Refashioning Ben Jonson: Gender, Politics, and the Jonsonian Canon*, St. Martin's Press, 1998.

Scherer, Jacques. *La dramaturgie classique en France*. 1950. Librairie Nizet, 2001.

Shannon, Laurie. *Sovereign Amity: Figures of Friendship in Shakespearean Contexts*. U of Chicago P, 2002.

Shapiro, James. *Rival Playwrights: Marlowe, Jonson, Shakespeare*. Columbia UP, 1991.

Spedding, James. *The Letters and the Life of Francis Bacon*. Vol. 6. Longmans, 1872.

Starkey, David, editor. *The English Court: From the Wars of the Roses to the Civil War*. Longman, 1987.

Steigerwald, Jörn. "Sujets de l'amour: forms de la re-présentation de soi dans la société de cour d'après *Le Favori*." *Madame de Villedieu et le théâtre*, edited by N. Grande and E. Keller-Rahbé, Narr, 2009, pp. 171–83.

Tacitus, Cornelius. *The Annals*. Edited by J. Yardley and A. Barrett, Oxford UP, 2008.

Taylor, Jennifer. *Lucy Countess of Bedford, Jonson, and Donne*. Dissertation, McMaster U, 1979.

Teasley, David. "The Charge of Sodomy as a Political Weapon in Early Modern France: The Case of Henry III in Catholic League Polemic, 1585–1589." *The Maryland Historian*, vol. 18, no. 1, 1987, pp. 17–30.

The Emperor's Favourite. Edited by Siobhan Keenan, Manchester UP, 2010.

The Tragedy of Tiberius. Edited by Walter W. Greg, Oxford UP, 1914.

Vawter, Marvin. "The Seeds of Virtue: Political Imperatives in Jonson's *Sejanus*." *Studies in the Literary Imagination*, vol. 6, no. 1, 1973, pp. 41–60.

Vega, Lope de. *La inocente sangre. Comedias. Parte XIX*. Juan González, 1624.

Vélez de Guevara, Luis. *El espejo del mundo*. Edited by William Manson and George Peale, introduction by Maria Grazia Profeti, Juan de la Cuesta, 2002.

Weimer, Christopher. "The (Homo)erotics of *Privanza*: The Count of Villamediana and Tirso's *Privar contra su gusto*." *Lesbianism and Homosexuality in Early Modern Spain: Literature and Theater in Context*, edited by M. J. Delgado and A. Saint-Saëns, UP of the South, 2000, pp. 257–74.

Wells, Robin, et al. *Neo-Historicism: Studies in Renaissance Literature, History, and Politics*, D.S. Brewer, 2000.

Worden, Blair. "A Frisson in the Auditorium." Review of *How Shakespeare Put Politics on the Stage: Power and Succession in the History Plays*, by Peter Lake. *London Review of Books*, vol. 39, no. 8, 2017, pp. 36–38.

———. "Ben Jonson among the Historians." *Culture and Politics in Early Stuart England*, edited by K. Sharpe and P. Lake, Stanford UP, 1993, pp. 67–89.

———. "Ben Jonson and the Monarchy." Wells et al., pp. 71–90.

———. "Favourites on the English Stage." Elliott and Brockliss, pp. 159–83.

Wright, Pam. "A Change in Direction: The Ramifications of a Female Household, 1558–1603." Starkey, pp. 147–72.

Conclusion

The appearance of royal favorites on stage coincides with the emergence of all-powerful ministers, such as the Duke of Lerma, the Cardinal Richelieu, and the Duke of Buckingham, in the monarchies of Spain, France, and England, respectively. Throughout the late sixteenth and seventeenth centuries, the favorite minister develops into a frequent character in numerous dramas and becomes the protagonist of at least 150 plays. These dramas that feature the character of a favorite, regardless of whether he is the protagonist, complement other theatrical representations of royal favoritism such as *autos sacramentales*, court ballets, and court masques.

This book has contributed to the enlargement of this group of dramas by analyzing an unedited play, *La paciencia en la fortuna*. This analysis has revealed the extraordinary importance of *La paciencia* due to two main reasons: first, the author of the play is arguably the prominent dramatist Lope de Vega, and second, the play adds useful information to the field of dramas on favorites not only in Spain, since it illustrates clearly how many Spanish dramatists used to depict royal favorites, but also in a wider European context. In order to delve into this last aspect, and with the aim of exploring the diversity of dramas featuring favorites across the three main European monarchies in the early modern period, *La paciencia* has been studied here in comparison with two plays dealing with the topic of favoritism and written by playwrights from France and England: Marie-Catherine Desjardins' *Le Favori, ou la Coquette* and Ben Jonson's *Sejanus His Fall*. The analysis of these three plays highlights some features that are shared among the vast and diverse group of dramas concerning favorites. These common features can be summarized as the paradox between past and present of these dramas, which as a rule comment on the contemporary political scene while they are set in distant places and times. The setting of both *La paciencia* and *Le Favori* is the medieval north-east of the Iberian Peninsula, while *Sejanus* is set in ancient Rome. The historical dimension of two of these plays is reinforced by the fact that their stories are alleged to be based on historiographical sources: a medieval chronicle, in the case of *La paciencia* (53v), and classical works, in the case of *Sejanus*. However, the approach of the authors of dramas on favorites to history is primarily rhetorical and has little interest to research or explain events from the past. Playwrights in the early modern age use history as a source of exempla to elaborate stories that always and inevitably include a commentary on the present. As such, *La paciencia*, *Le Favori*, and *Sejanus*, without being *pièces à clef*, echo contemporary views of political favoritism, and the protagonists of these plays are, to some extent, reminiscent of the favorite ministers of their time.

The political immediacy of dramas on favorites often had specific purposes as a consequence of the literary patronage that was commonplace in the early modern courts. The establishment of patronage relationships between dramatists and powerful courtiers responded to a mutual interest, since the latter provided protection and favors to playwrights, who, in exchange, offered a cultural product that could serve as both entertainment and propaganda for patrons. In this regard, royal favorites, as the greatest court patrons, due to their unique position in the monarch's highest favor, were extraordinary promoters of theatrical activities as well as the center of dramatic praise. Of the three principal dramas analyzed in this book, *La paciencia* is the play that most clearly shows the playwright's purpose to eulogize the figure of a royal favorite, the Duke of Lerma. This play forms part of a propagandistic campaign to defend the position of Lerma and, more particularly, is associated with a larger group of Spanish dramas intended to emphasize the positive virtues of the king's favorite minister. Some of these dramas were commissioned by Lerma himself to be performed in his several residencies at special events. Lope de Vega, who was linked to the favorite's client network by patronage relationships, was a regular dramatist at those events. *La paciencia* appears to celebrate the wedding of Lerma's relatives (Gómez) and belongs to that category of dramas reflecting the playwrights' relationships of patronage. *Sejanus* is also an example of this type of drama. Even though the Earl of Essex had already passed away when the play was first performed in 1603, *Sejanus* is a product of the culture of the Essex faction and reflects the political sentiments of this court faction in which Ben Jonson, at that time, found his literary patrons. Likewise, in *Le Favori*, which may be the only play written by a female dramatist during the seventeenth century that portrays a favorite, Desjardins gives prominence to the character of Lindamire, who bears significant resemblances to the playwright's friend and literary patron, the powerful Grande Mademoiselle.

The success of the three aforementioned playwrights, who wrote to make their living and to establish their status in court society, depended largely on their relations of patronage. This dependency provides an explanation for the abandonment of the theater by Desjardins, who failed to find the required support to continue her career as a dramatist. In contrast, Lope de Vega and Ben Jonson forged more fruitful relationships with their patrons, and both became successful court dramatists who entertained and praised their patrons under the protection of favorite ministers. Lope de Vega (1562–1635) and Ben Jonson (1572–1637) were contemporaries, and their backgrounds and careers share close resemblances. They were born in humble circumstances and served in the military before they began to write plays. In both cases, their beginnings as playwrights, during the reigns of Philip II and Elizabeth I, were characterized by problems with the authorities. Their situation improved significantly upon the accession of new monarchs and the further development of political favoritism. Both Lope and Jonson aspired to be the new Virgil or Horace of Philip III and James I, who were compared to Emperor Augustus (Wright; Pierce). This goal was to a great extent achieved, since their dramatic work was widely recognized. However, this fame left their financial problems unresolved, and Lope and Jonson were forced to continue writing and counting on their patrons' subsidies until the end of their lives (Martínez, esp. 531–649, Donaldson, esp. 399–428).

The relations implicit in a system of patronage, therefore, are a decisive factor for understanding and interpreting dramas on favorites. Another important factor, which is also common to these dramas across Spain, France, and England, is the Neostoic philosophy that began to spread in the late sixteenth century mainly through the works of Justus Lipsius. This Neostoicism is broadly understood as a combination of the Stoicism of authors such as Seneca with both Christian principles and Tacitus' views on history and politics. The three plays studied in this book are indebted to Neostoicism, while reflecting its impact differently in each work.

La paciencia features a royal favorite who adheres to the Stoic virtue of patience and remains loyal to an apparently unjust King, similar to a martyr who suffers the pains by which God tests his faith. This Stoic and Christian representation of favoritism is also seen, although in a lesser degree, in *Le Favori*. In this play, not only are the Stoic values of the favorite overshadowed by those of Lindamire but also the virtuous faction that Moncade forms with Lindamire and Alvar is challenged by a "chameleonic" group of courtiers who repudiate the principles of Stoicism. In both *La paciencia* and *Le Favori*, the moral philosophy of Seneca is the main source of inspiration, and this inclination may reflect a more general preference for the moralist Seneca among Spanish and French playwrights who stage favorites. In Spain, a widespread tendency to highlight the virtues of royal favorites, among other factors, explains the importance of Stoicism in dramas on favorites, especially in those written by Lope de Vega, who showed little interest in Tacitus (Jameson; Blanco and Sánchez) and much in Seneca (Albrecht). In France in the 1630s and 1640s there is a trend of plays related to ancient Rome, such as Pierre Corneille's *Cinna*, in which Seneca and his moral philosophy are a prime source. Moreover, these plays tend to focus on a glorious age of the Roman history, based on the ancient and honorable values that are highlighted by historians such as Livy and Plutarch. The influence of Tacitus and the depiction of a decadent Rome in French dramas take place decades later in the century, especially in the dramatic work of Jean Racine, but also of Corneille, who uses Tacitus to write the play concerning favorites *Othon* (Sweetser). *Le Favori*, which was written at the exact same time as *Othon* (1664), echoes the Stoic tradition of Corneille's classical dramas and, at the same time, introduces elements of a more modern and cynical view of court life as represented by Tacitus.

In *Sejanus*, Tacitus' *Annals* is not only the primary source of information but also a work that models Jonson's view of political favoritism as the product of a society devoid of values in which Stoic principles are rendered as mere hypocrisy. The setting of *Sejanus* is the urban and corrupt environment of the court; unlike *La paciencia* and *Le Favori*, Jonson's play includes no scenes of nature in which the royal favorites of the two other dramas cultivate their virtues. Thus Jonson's approach to favoritism in *Sejanus* contrasts with that of Desjardins and especially with Lope's portrayal of a remarkably virtuous favorite in *La paciencia*, even though the same intellectual tradition, Neostoicism, informs the three dramatists. This diverse treatment of favoritism in drama is not only a consequence of prioritizing various Neostoic sources such as Seneca in *La paciencia* and Tacitus in *Sejanus*; the images of favorites depicted in these dramas are also conditioned by the patronage relationships of the playwrights, as already mentioned. Furthermore, one can further expand on the differences between national dramas and concentrate on the tendency of English plays, such as Jonson's *Sejanus*, to depict favorite ministers negatively, which appears less frequently in Spanish and French theater. However, this method of analysis based on national divisions fails to fully comprehend the diversity of dramas on favorites. For instance, Lope de Vega also staged wicked favorites, such as the character Don Egas in *El Duque de Viseo*, a play that has been read in light of Lipsius' Tacitism (Campbell). In addition, the transgressive nature of Sejanus was also explored by Spanish and French dramatists such as Pérez de Montalbán and Cyrano de Bergerac.

A more direct way to approach the study of dramas on favorites across Europe is to analyze the themes and concepts that they share. In this regard, scholars focus largely on the topic of Fortune and the *de casibus* structure of the rise and fall of favorites that is associated with Fortune's fluctuations. However, in the various plays analyzed here, Fortune, for instance, is by no means a determining factor in the course of actions, and only *Sejanus* shows the expected fall of a favorite. These conclusions, in turn, can be extended to many other dramas on favorites that fail to include either the ascension or the downfall of a favorite minister and in which Fortune plays a minor role such as *Cómo ha de ser el privado*, *Clitandre*, or *The Deserving Favourite*.

This book has paid particular attention to Neostoicism, which, due to its wide diffusion in early modern Europe, its contribution to shaping images of political favoritism, as well as the diversity of its sources and concepts, is probably the most inclusive theoretical framework for the analysis of dramas on favorites. Even the notion of Fortune, as opposed to virtue, falls into the area of Neostoic discussion. More importantly, the Neostoic theory also includes a reflection on the paradox between past and present characteristic of dramas on favorites, as Lipsius famously insisted on comparing the imperial Rome of favorite ministers to "a theater of our modern life."

Works Cited

Albrecht, Jane. "Stoicism, Seneca and Seventeenth-Century Spanish Tragedy." Scripta Humanistica, 2012.

Blanco, Emilio, and Antonio Sánchez. "Lope de Vega, en la encrucijada de la novela (corta): sentencias y aforismos en las *Novelas a Marcia Leonarda* (1621 y 1624)." *Revista de filología española*, vol. 96, no. 1, 2016, pp. 39–59.

Campbell, Ysla. "*El Duque de Viseo* y las *Políticas* de Justo Lipsio." *Nuevos caminos del hispanismo...: Actas del XVI Congreso de la Asociación Internacional de Hispanistas*, vol. 2, edited by P. Civil and F. Crémoux, Iberoamericana, 2010, accessed 20 March, 2020, https://cvc.cervantes.es/literatura/aih/pdf/16/aih_16_2_059.pdf

Corneille, Pierre. *Cinna*. Edited by Alain Riffaud, Droz, 2011.

Desjardins, Marie-Catherine (Madame de Villedieu). *Le Favori*. Edited by Delphine Amstutz, Hermann, 2017.

Donaldson, Ian. *Ben Jonson: A Life*. Oxford UP, 2011.

Gómez Martos, Francisco. "*La paciencia en la fortuna*: An Unprinted Play by Lope de Vega". *Arte nuevo. Revista de estudios áureos*, vol. 6, 2019, pp. 57–89.

Jameson, Ann. "Lope de Vega's knowledge of classical literature." *Bulletin Hispanique*, vol. 38, no. 4, 1936, pp. 444–501.

Jonson, Ben. *Sejanus His Fall*. Edited by Tom Cain. *The Cambridge Edition of the Works of Ben Jonson*, 7 vols., edited by D. Bevington et al., Cambridge UP, 2012, vol. 2, pp. 195–391.

La paciencia en la fortuna. CC*IV 28033, *Comedias de Diferentes Autores*, vol. 74, no. 2. Biblioteca Palatina di Parma, Parma. 1–55r.

Martínez, José Florencio. *Biografía de Lope de Vega (1562–1635): Un friso literario del Siglo de Oro*. PPU, 2011.

Pierce, Robert. "Ben Jonson's Horace and Horace's Ben Jonson." *Studies in Philology*, vol. 78, no. 1, 1981, pp. 20–31.

Sweetser, Marie-Odile. "Racine rival de Corneille: 'Innutrition' et innovations dans *Britannicus*." *Romanic Review*, vol. 66, no. 1, 1975, pp. 13–31.

Tacitus, Cornelius. *The Annals*. Edited by J. Yardley and A. Barrett. Oxford UP, 2008.

Vega, Lope de. *El duque de Viseo*. Edited by M. Calderón. *Comedias de Lope de Vega. Parte VI*. Vol. 2, edited by V. Pineda and G. Pontón, Milenio, 2005, pp. 1031–60.

Wright, Elizabeth. *Pilgrimage to Patronage: Lope de Vega and the Court of Philip III, 1598–1621*. Bucknell UP, 2001.

Index

Note: Page numbers followed by 'n' refer to end notes.

www.ingramcontent.com/pod-product-compliance
Lightning Source LLC
LaVergne TN
LVHW021112300926
849160LV00009B/704
* 9 7 8 0 3 6 7 5 3 8 4 3 9 *